ILLUSTRATED LIBRARY OF COOKING

VOLUME 5 Chi-Coo

In this volume: *a cookbook
for children with recipes for
the littlest cook, the
intermediate and the advanced
that features a sugarplum
land full of storybook treats
to shape and bake . . .
hearty dishes to warm
wintry days and refreshing
fare to cool summer
sizzlers . . . plus a jumbo-size
cookie book with dozens
of round-the-world recipes
you may not know.*

ROCKVILLE HOUSE PUBLISHERS, INC.
ROCKVILLE CENTRE, NEW YORK 11570

Family Circle.

Illustrated Library of

COOKING

YOUR READY REFERENCE FOR A LIFETIME OF GOOD EATING

Picture Credits:

American Spice Trade Association • Best Foods, a Division of CPC International • Peanut Growers of Georgia and Alabama • The Chocolate Information Council • The Kitchens of Hawaiian Punch • The Nestle Company Inc.

Heat-beater: a cool fruit soup afloat with raspberries, peaches.

Table of Contents

CHILDREN'S HOUR:
NO-COOK RECIPES SMALL
CHILDREN CAN MAKE, THE WAY TO
SUGARPLUM LAND, A GROWN-UP
MEAL CHILDREN CAN MAKE

Kitchens just naturally attract children. There are spoons and bowls to lick, cookies to snitch and maybe a batter to beat or cake to frost. Very early, little girls long to cook (boys, too). And wise the mother who encourages them.

Small children can be started on no-cook cookies and candies. They will love working the mixtures with their hands, feeling it squish through their fingers (much better than mud pies because these are for real and can be eaten!). By the time children have reached school age, they are ready for actual cooking— for frying eggs, perhaps, stirring together a batch of pancakes or whipping up mounds of cookie dough which they can then shape and decorate to their hearts' delight.

Once a child has learned the basic techniques, he is ready to move on—to a whole meal perhaps, a very grown-up meal that he can actually plan and prepare solo.

The recipes included here offer something for every young cook—the beginner, the intermediate and the advanced. It's hoped they will teach the child both the fun and fascination of food and tempt him to try more advanced recipes included in the other volumes of THE FAMILY CIRCLE ILLUSTRATED LIBRARY OF COOKING.

◄ *Decorated cookie cut-outs allow children to develop their culinary and artistic skills at the same time.*

NO-COOK RECIPES SMALL CHILDREN CAN MAKE

Tiny Tree Sandwiches
Makes 2 dozen small sandwiches

1 *loaf (18 slices) thin-sliced white bread*
4 *tablespoons (½ stick) softened butter or margarine*
   HAM FILLING *(recipe follows)*
   CHEESE FILLING *(recipe follows)*

1 Spread bread slices with softened butter or margarine; arrange in 3 rows of 6 slices each; spread first row with HAM FILLING; cover with slices in second row, butter side down; spread unbuttered sides with CHEESE FILLING; top with remaining slices, butter side down, to make 6 sandwiches; wrap in wax paper, aluminum foil, or transparent food wrap; chill.
2 To make trees: Unwrap sandwiches; trim crusts; cut each sandwich diagonally to make 4 triangles; run a wooden pick through middle slice of each, from center of long side to point opposite.

   HAM FILLING—Combine 1 small can (4½ ounces) deviled ham with 2 teaspoons mayonnaise or salad dressing, and ½ teaspoon prepared mustard in small bowl. Makes about ⅓ cup.
   CHEESE FILLING—Cream 1 package (3 to 4 ounces) cream cheese with 1 tablespoon grated

519

Parmesan cheese, 1 teaspoon lemon juice, and ⅛ teaspoon Worcestershire sauce to spreading consistency in small bowl. Makes about ⅓ cup.

Choco-Banana Pops
Makes 1 dozen

    1 package (6 ounces) semisweet-chocolate
      pieces
    6 firm ripe bananas
    12 long wooden skewers

1 Melt semisweet-chocolate pieces in top of double boiler over simmering water; remove from heat but keep hot over hot water.
2 Peel bananas; cut in half crosswise; insert a skewer into each.
3 Frost each half with melted chocolate, holding by its skewer handle; place in a single layer in a chilled buttered shallow pan.
4 Freeze 2 to 3 hours, or until firm. Slip a fluted paper baking cup or a paper napkin onto handle of each "lollipop" before serving.

Prune Clusters
Little cooks can make these chocolate fruit-and-nut candies once the chopping's done—they're that easy.
Makes 3 dozen

    1 cup (6-ounce package) semisweet-chocolate
      pieces
    1 cup finely cut pitted dried prunes (from a
      12-ounce package)
    ½ cup coarsely chopped salted peanuts
    ½ cup flaked coconut
    ½ cup finely chopped salted peanuts

1 Melt semisweet-chocolate pieces in top of double boiler over hot water. Remove from heat; stir in prunes and coarsely chopped peanuts until fruit and nuts are well-coated.
2 Sprinkle coconut and finely chopped peanuts on separate sheets of wax paper or foil. Drop half of prune mixture, a teaspoonful at a time, onto coconut; roll into balls. Place in single layer on cookie sheet. Repeat with remaining prune mixture, rolling in peanuts. Chill all until firm.

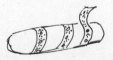

520

Sparkles
Makes about 1½ pounds candy

    1 package (about 11 ounces) mixed dried fruits
    1 jar (8 ounces) mixed candied fruits
    1 can flaked coconut
    2 tablespoons lemon juice
      Sugar
      Small red and green gumdrops

1 Put dried and candied fruits through food chopper, using fine blade; add coconut and lemon juice; mix well.
2 Form into small patties; dust with sugar and decorate with a red or green gumdrop. OR: Shape into 1½-inch-long rolls; dust with sugar and add a cut red gumdrop "flame."

Batons
Another shaping project for six-year-olds.
Makes about 5 dozen cookies

    1 package (4¾ ounces) vanilla wafers
    ½ cup finely chopped pecans
    ½ cup sifted 10X (confectioners' powdered)
      sugar
    ¼ teaspoon cinnamon
    1½ tablespoons light corn syrup
    ¼ cup canned pineapple juice
      VANILLA FROSTING (recipe follows)
      Multicolor sprinkles

1 Roll vanilla wafers fine; combine with pecans, sugar, cinnamon, corn syrup, and pineapple juice in medium-size bowl; blend well.
2 Form into thin 2-inch-long sticks by rolling between palms of hands; place on cookie sheets covered with wax paper or foil; let dry overnight.
3 To decorate: Dip ends of batons in VANILLA FROSTING, then into multicolor sprinkles.

   VANILLA FROSTING—Blend 1 cup sifted confectioners' (powdered) sugar, 1 tablespoon water, and ½ teaspoon vanilla in small bowl.

Pink Almond Pearls
You do the mincing, let the children do the mixing.
Makes about 8 dozen

    1 can (8 ounces) almond paste

1 cup sifted 10X (confectioners' powdered) sugar
2 tablespoons water
½ cup finely chopped seedless raisins
½ cup finely chopped dried apricots
1 teaspoon rum flavoring or extract
½ teaspoon vanilla
PINK ICING (recipe follows)

1 Combine almond paste, 10X sugar, water, raisins, apricots, rum flavoring or extract, and vanilla in a medium-size bowl; mix with a fork to blend completely. (Mixture will be stiff.)
2 Roll, 1 teaspoonful at a time, into marble-size balls between palms of hands.
3 Drop each into PINK ICING; lift out with a fork and hold over bowl to let excess icing drip back. Place balls, not touching, on wire racks set over wax paper or foil; let stand 2 to 3 hours, or until icing is firm. (Scrape any icing that drips onto paper or foil back into bowl to use again.) Store balls in a single layer in a covered container.

PINK ICING—Beat 1 egg white slightly in a small bowl. Beat in ½ teaspoon white vinegar, then 1¾ cups 10X (confectioners' powdered) sugar with an electric or rotary beater. Continue beating 10 minutes, or until icing is thick and fluffy. Tint delicate pink with a few drops red food coloring. Makes about 1 cup.

No-Cook Bonbons
Can't-fail, easy way to make luscious creamy fondant.
Makes about 2 pounds

¼ cup (½ stick) butter or margarine
5 to 6 cups sifted 10X (confectioners' powdered) sugar
1 egg white
3 tablespoons evaporated milk
Few drops almond extract
Green food coloring
Few drops oil of wintergreen
Red food coloring
Few drops oil of peppermint

1 Cream butter or margarine until soft in large bowl; blend in 2 cups sugar and unbeaten egg white.
2 Blend in evaporated milk and rest of sugar, adding only enough sugar to make fondant easy to handle. (Mixture will be soft, yet firm enough to knead without crumbling.)
3 Turn out on board lightly dusted with 10X sugar; knead until smooth and even-textured; divide into thirds.
4 Knead almond extract into one portion; color second portion light green with green food coloring and knead in oil of wintergreen, drop by drop, to flavor lightly; color remaining portion pink with red food coloring and flavor with oil of peppermint. Shape as follows:

PINK SNOWBALLS—Mold small pieces of peppermint fondant into small balls; coat with coconut.

NOEL PATTIES—Shape almond fondant into 1-inch rounds; decorate tops with (1) walnut halves; (2) cut candied cherries and green gumdrops or angelica; (3) almonds tipped with melted chocolate; or (4) tinted sugar.

CHRISTMAS TREES—Mold small pieces of wintergreen fondant with fingers into tree shapes; roll each in multicolor sprinkles; top with a silver candy; stand on a NOEL PATTY.

ALMOND DATES—Stuff pitted dates with almond fondant; leave plain or roll in granulated sugar.

TWINKLES—Roll out almond fondant ¼ inch thick on board lightly dusted with 10X sugar; cut part with small star-shape cutter, rest with small Christmas-tree-ball cardboard pattern. Decorate stars with crushed peppermint-stick candy; balls with multicolor sprinkles and silver candy (clean tweezers are a help).

Choco-Peanut Fudge
In this no-cook treat, peanut butter blends with chocolate for the mellowest flavor.
Makes about 2 pounds

1 package (12 ounces) semisweet-chocolate pieces
½ cup smooth peanut butter
3 cups sifted 10X (confectioners' powdered) sugar
½ cup milk

1 Melt chocolate pieces in the top of a double boiler over simmering water; remove from heat.
2 Blend in peanut butter, then beat in 10X sugar and milk until smooth. Spread in a buttered pan, 8x8x2.
3 Chill at least ½ hour, or until firm. Cut into 1-inch squares. Cover and store at room temperature.

THE WAY TO SUGARPLUM LAND

Dreamland Cut-outs

Finnish children call these thin crisp spicy ginger cookies piparkakut.
Bake at 350° for 7 minutes. Makes 1½ dozen large and 6 dozen tiny cut-outs, plus 5 dozen round cookies

¾ cup molasses
1 teaspoon grated orange rind
1 teaspoon ground cinnamon
1 teaspoon ground ginger
⅛ teaspoon ground cloves
4 cups sifted all-purpose flour
1 teaspoon baking soda
¼ teaspoon salt
½ cup (1 stick) butter or margarine
¼ cup sugar
1 egg
ORNAMENTAL FROSTING (recipe follows)

1 Combine molasses, orange rind, cinnamon, ginger, and cloves in a small saucepan; heat, stirring constantly, just to boiling; cool.
2 Measure flour, soda, and salt into sifter.
3 Cream butter or margarine with sugar until fluffy in a large bowl; beat in egg and cooled molasses mixture.
4 Sift in dry ingredients, a third at a time, blending well to make a stiff dough. Chill several hours, overnight, or until firm enough to roll.
5 Divide dough in half; wrap one half in wax paper, foil, or transparent wrap and chill for making round cookies in Step 7. Divide remaining dough into quarters, for it's easier to roll a small amount at a time. Return three quarters to refrigerator.
6 Roll out dough *very thin* on a lightly floured pastry cloth or board. Cut out fancy cookies using homemade cardboard pattern or your favorite cookie cutters, floured. Transfer with spatula to ungreased cookie sheets. Roll and cut out remaining three quarters of chilled dough this same way.
7 Use wrapped half of dough for round cookies, using an about-2-inch cutter.
8 Bake all in moderate oven (350°) 7 minutes, or until firm. Remove from cookie sheets; cool completely on wire racks.
9 Decorate with plain or tinted ORNAMENTAL FROSTING. Leave round cookies plain, or frost, as you wish.

522

An enchanting, cookie snowscape children can make.

Ornamental Frosting

Store any leftover frosting in a covered jar in the refrigerator for another day's baking.
Makes about ¾ cup

 1 *egg white*
 ⅛ *teaspoon cream of tartar*
 ⅛ *teaspoon vanilla*
 1¾ *cups sifted 10X (confectioners' powdered) sugar*

1 Beat egg white, cream of tartar, and vanilla until foamy in a small bowl. Beat in 10X sugar gradually until frosting stands in firm peaks and is stiff enough to hold a sharp line when cut through with a knife.
2 Use plain or divide into custard cups and tint with food colorings, if you wish.

Hansel and Gretel Cookies

These storybook favorites will delight children of all ages.
Bake at 350° for 12 minutes. Makes six 7-inch cookies

 1½ *cups sifted all-purpose flour*
 ½ *teaspoon baking powder*
 ¼ *teaspoon salt*
 ½ *cup (1 stick) butter or margarine*
 ½ *cup sugar*
 1 *egg*
 ½ *teaspoon vanilla*
 ½ *teaspoon orange extract*
 1 *recipe* ORNAMENTAL FROSTING *(recipe precedes)*
 Red, green, and yellow food colorings

1 Measure flour, baking powder, and salt into sifter.
2 Cream butter or margarine with sugar until fluffy in a medium-size bowl; beat in egg, vanilla, and orange extract.
3 Sift in dry ingredients, half at a time, blending well to make a stiff dough. Chill several hours, overnight, or until firm enough to roll.
4 Make cardboard patterns of a boy and a girl, each 7 inches tall, following the simple outlines pictured in the photograph. (Or use a large gingerbread-man cookie cutter.)
5 Roll out half of dough at a time, ¼ inch thick, on a lightly floured pastry cloth or board.
6 Lay cardboard pattern for boy on dough and cut out 3 cookie shapes with a sharp knife; place on ungreased cookie sheet. Repeat with remaining half of dough and pattern for girl. (Reroll and bake trimmings for cookie-jar treats.)
7 Bake in moderate oven (350°) 12 minutes, or until firm and delicately golden. Remove from cookie sheets; cool completely on wire racks.
8 Make ORNAMENTAL FROSTING and divide among 4 custard cups; leave one white; then tint remaining pink, green, and yellow with food colorings. Fit writing tip onto a cake-decorating set; fill with frostings, one color at a time; decorate cookies as pictured. (To decorate quickly with colored frostings of your choice, buy decorating frostings in pressurized cans. Each can comes with a set of decorating tips.

Peppermint Shrubs

Makes 1 dozen small shrubs

 ⅔ *cup sugar*
 ⅔ *cup light corn syrup*
 ½ *teaspoon salt*
 ½ *teaspoon peppermint extract*
 Green food coloring
 4 *cups puffed-rice cereal*

1 Combine sugar, corn syrup, salt, and peppermint extract in a large saucepan; tint a delicate green with food coloring. Heat slowly, stirring constantly, just until sugar dissolves. Remove from heat.
2 Stir in cereal; toss with a wooden spoon until evenly coated. Cook, stirring constantly, over medium heat 5 minutes, or until mixture is very sticky.
3 Turn out onto a large sheet of wax paper or foil; let stand a few minutes to cool. (Cereal stays sticky enough to mold even when cool.)
4 Press into small rounds or pyramids to resemble shrubs or bushes. Set on wax paper or foil to dry.
5 Leave plain or, for a snowy look, brush very lightly with light corn syrup and sprinkle with grated coconut.

Popcorn Poplars

Youngsters can make a whole forest of these good-to-eat trees. For easy handling, work with one recipe at a time.
Makes 1 tree

 ⅓ *cup sugar*
 ⅓ *cup light corn syrup*
 ¼ *teaspoon salt*
 ½ *teaspoon vanilla*
 Green food coloring

524

4 cups unsalted freshly popped popcorn
1 twelve-inch-long thin dowel stick
FANTASTIC, FAST FUDGE *base (recipe follows)*

1 Combine sugar, corn syrup, salt, and vanilla in a large saucepan; tint a delicate green with food coloring. Heat slowly, stirring constantly, just until sugar dissolves. Remove from heat.
2 Stir in popped corn; toss with a wooden spoon until evenly coated. Cook, stirring constantly, over medium heat, 5 minutes, or until mixture is very sticky.
3 Turn out onto a large sheet of wax paper or foil; let stand a few minutes to cool. (Popcorn stays sticky enough to mold even when cool.)
4 Press around dowel stick to make a "tree" about 11 inches tall and 2½ inches at base. Set on wax paper or foil to dry. To hold tree upright, "plant" it in a cup filled with FANTASTIC, FAST FUDGE.

Lollipop Garden
Gaily colored candy flowers bloom in this garden of rich creamy fudge.
Makes 1 garden of 24 pops and 1 block of fudge

24 sipper straws
   Assorted ring-shape candies, nonpareils, and cream peppermints
1 cup sugar
½ cup light corn syrup
   Dash of salt
¼ cup water
⅛ teaspoon red food coloring
   FANTASTIC, FAST FUDGE BASE *(recipe follows)*
   ORNAMENTAL FROSTING *(recipe precedes)*

1 Place sipper straws, 3 inches apart, on well-buttered cookie sheets. Place a candy about ¼ inch above one end of each straw.
2 Combine sugar, corn syrup, salt, and water in a medium-size heavy saucepan. Heat slowly, stirring constantly, until sugar dissolves, then cook, without stirring, to 300° on a candy thermometer. (A teaspoon of syrup dropped into cold water will separate right away into threads that are hard and brittle.)
3 Drop syrup mixture by tablespoonfuls over candy at ends of half of the straws to form 2-inch round lollipops. Work quickly, and if syrup thickens too soon, reheat slowly, stirring constantly, just until syrupy again. Stir red food coloring into remaining syrup mixture to tint bright red. Drop over remaining candies and straws. Let cool on cookie sheets until firm.
4 Make FANTASTIC, FAST FUDGE and mold in a loaf pan, 7½x3¾x2¼.

5 When ready to put garden together, cover a piece of cardboard about 7x3 with foil for base. Loosen fudge around edge of pan with knife; turn out onto base.
6 Make ORNAMENTAL FROSTING. Spoon into a cake-decorating set. Using small round tip, pipe frosting onto edge of fudge to look like a fence. (Or use a decorating frosting in a pressurized can or plastic tube, if you wish.)
7 Press lollipop "flowers" in fudge base, cutting some of the straws so flowers will be different heights.

Fantastic, Fast Fudge
Makes about 1 pound

2 packages (6 ounces each) semisweet chocolate pieces
⅔ cup plus 2 tablespoons sweetened condensed milk
   Pinch of salt
1 teaspoon vanilla extract

1 Place chocolate pieces in the top part of a double boiler and set over boiling water; heat and stir until chocolate pieces are melted; remove from heat.
2 Stir in sweetened condensed milk, salt and vanilla and mix only until smooth.
3 Turn into a wax paper-lined pan and press into a block about 1-inch thick, or shape as directed for LOLLIPOP GARDEN *(recipe precedes)*. Chill in the refrigerator about 2 hours until firm.
4 Remove pan from refrigerator and turn upside-down on a cutting board. Peel off wax paper. Cut or shape fudge as desired, or press into cups to make bases for POPCORN POPLARS *(recipe precedes)*.

Snowcap Cookie Cottage
Build this little cottage of chocolate-walnut cookie dough to admire first, then eat within two or three days.
Bake at 375° for 20 minutes. Makes 1 cookie house

3½ cups sifted all-purpose flour
1½ teaspoons baking soda
1 teaspoon salt
¾ cup (1½ sticks) butter or margarine
¾ cup vegetable shortening
1 cup granulated sugar
1 cup firmly packed brown sugar
3 eggs
1 teaspoon vanilla

525

3 packages (6 ounces each) semisweet-chocolate pieces
1½ cups chopped walnuts (from an 8-ounce can)
FLUFFY FROSTING (recipe follows)
Green decorating sugar
Silver and red candies
Birthday-cake candles

1 Grease a baking pan, 15x10x1; line with wax paper; grease paper.
2 Measure flour, soda, and salt into sifter.
3 Cream butter or margarine and shortening with granulated and brown sugars until fluffy in a large bowl; beat in eggs and vanilla. Sift in dry ingredients, a third at a time, blending well to make a soft dough. Stir in semi-sweet-chocolate pieces and nuts.
4 Measure out 3 cups of dough and spread in prepared pan. (Set remaining dough aside for a second baking.)
5 Bake in moderate oven (375°) 20 minutes, or until top springs back when lightly pressed with fingertip. Cool in pan on wire rack 5 minutes; loosen around edge with knife; invert onto wire rack; peel off wax paper; cool layer completely.
6 Wash, dry, and prepare pan as in Step 1; spread remaining dough in pan; bake and cool as in Step 5.
7 Make house: Cover a piece of heavy cardboard, 8x6 inches, with foil for base of house.
8 Cut one cookie layer, following Diagram A, into 2 pieces, each 9x4 inches, for roof; 1 piece, 6x7 inches, for one end; and 2 squares, each 1½ inches, for front and back of chimney.

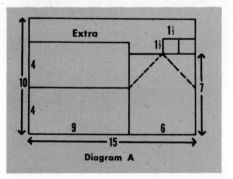

Diagram A

9 Cut second cookie layer, following Diagram B, into 2 pieces, each 8x4 inches, for side walls; 1 piece, 6x7 inches, for other end; and 2 pieces, each 1¾x2 inches, for sides of chimney. Trim the two 6x7-inch pieces as marked with dotted lines in diagrams to make slanted roof. Cut a wedge-shape piece 1 inch deep out of bottom of the two side chimney pieces so chimney will fit over roof. Cut 2 windows and a door in front

wall, 2 windows in back, and 2 in each of the end walls.

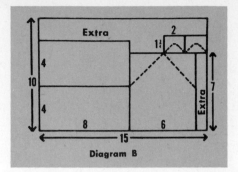

Diagram B

10 Make FLUFFY FROSTING. Spread part on side edges of front and back walls. Stand upright on cardboard base and hold in place, pressing on end walls firmly, and adding more frosting, if needed, to form shell of house. Hold in place a few minutes, then let stand 15 minutes to dry.
11 Spread top edge of front wall and slanted edges of end walls with frosting; set half of roof in place; hold a few minutes, then let stand 5 minutes. Set other section of roof in place the same way. Let house stand 15 minutes to dry completely.
12 Put chimney together with frosting, keeping straight edges even. Let stand, top down, 15 minutes, then set in place on roof.
13 When ready to decorate outside of house, beat 1 to 2 teaspoons water into remaining frosting to soften enough to give a drifted-snow effect. Spoon into a cake-decorating set. Using writing tip, pipe ribbons across roof to resemble shingles. Change to large round tip and press out frosting generously around chimney, door, windows, corners of house, and edges of roof, letting some drip down for "icicles." Trim door with a frosting "tree;" sprinkle with green sugar; outline with silver candies and place a red candy on top. Stand candles in windows.

FLUFFY FROSTING—Beat 3 egg whites with ¼ teaspoon cream of tartar and 1 teaspoon vanilla until foamy-white and double in volume in a large bowl. Beat in 6 cups (about 1½ packages) sifted 10X (confectioners' powdered) sugar very slowly until frosting stands in soft peaks and holds a line when cut through with a knife.

●

A GINGERBREAD CHURCH CHILDREN CAN BUILD

From the oven comes a most enchanting Christmas scene—a gingerbread church, horse and carriage and evergreen trees. With a candle

Easier to make than it looks, a gingerbread church with rock candy rose window and white frosting trim.

inside, shafts of light stream through the sugar-crystal stained windows.

Gingerbread Dough
Bake at 300° for 20 minutes. Makes 1 church, 1 sleigh, 2 horses, 2 large trees and 2 small trees

5½ *cups sifted all-purpose flour*
1 *teaspoon baking soda*
1 *teaspoon salt*
3 *teaspoons ground cinnamon*
2 *teaspoons ground ginger*
2 *teaspoons ground cloves*
1 *teaspoon ground nutmeg*
1 *cup vegetable shortening*
1 *cup sugar*
1 *cup molasses*
1 *egg*

1 Sift flour, baking soda, salt, cinnamon, ginger, cloves, and nutmeg onto wax paper.
2 Beat shortening with sugar until fluffy-light in a large bowl. Beat in molasses and egg. Stir in flour mixture to make a stiff dough. Chill several hours or overnight, until firm enough to roll.
3 Line a cookie sheet with aluminum foil; sprinkle lightly with flour. Roll out ¼ of the dough to a ⅛-inch thickness on foil. (This should cover the entire cookie sheet.)
4 Arrange as many pattern pieces as possible on dough, allowing at least ½ inch between

527

pieces; cut out pieces with a sharp knife. Carefully lift away all dough trims and save for rerolls.
5 Bake in very slow oven (300°) 20 minutes, or until cookies feel firm to the touch. Remove cookie sheet from oven and trim any cookie edges that are not straight while cookies are still warm. Cool cookies on cookie sheet on a wire rack for 5 minutes, then slide off foil and cool completely.
Note: If cookie pieces should break while assembling, simply put together with "cement" and cover with ROYAL FROSTING as part of the decoration.

Royal Frosting
Makes enough to decorate church, sleigh, horses, 2 large trees and 2 small trees

> 2 *egg whites*
> 1 *teaspoon lemon juice*
> 3½ *cups sifted 10X (confectioners' powdered) sugar*
> *Blue, green, and yellow food coloring*

Beat egg whites and lemon juice until foamy in a medium-size bowl. Slowly beat in sugar, until frosting stands in firm peaks and is stiff enough to hold a sharp line when cut through with a knife. Divide half the frosting among 3 small bowls. Tint one blue, one green, and one yellow with food colorings. Leave remaining half of frosting white. Keep all frostings covered with damp paper toweling to keep from drying until ready to use.

Sugar "Cement"
Spread 1 cup sugar in a small heavy skillet; heat slowly until sugar melts and starts to turn pale golden in color. Use immediately.

Church with Rose Window
GINGERBREAD DOUGH
Rock candy crystals
Red food coloring
Sugar "Cement"
Royal Frosting

1 Cut out GINGERBREAD DOUGH, following pattern directions for church. Press pieces of rock candy into dough to form the "stained glass" effect; brush red food coloring on rock candy to tint.
2 Bake and cool, following cookie dough directions.
3 To assemble: Dip the edge of cookie pieces into "cement," then quickly press together, following diagram.

4 Fit a pastry bag with a small star tip; fill bag and decorate with ROYAL FROSTING.

Christmas Trees
GINGERBREAD DOUGH
ROYAL FROSTING

1 Cut out GINGERBREAD DOUGH, following pattern directions for large and small trees. Bake and cool, following cookie dough directions.
2 As soon as cookies come out of oven, trim cut-out slots if they have filled in while baking.
3 Fit trees together.
4 Decorate with ROYAL FROSTING.

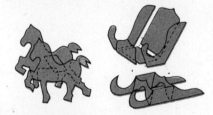

Sleigh and Horses
GINGERBREAD DOUGH
ROYAL FROSTING

1 Cut out GINGERBREAD DOUGH, following pattern directions for sleigh and horses.
2 Bake, following cookie dough directions. As soon as cookies come out of the oven, remove sleigh front and lay over the side of a small jar to give the curve for sleigh front.

528

3 To assemble: Dip the edge of cookie pieces into "cement" and press together, following assembly diagram for sleigh.
4 Dip second sleigh bottom into "cement" and press together, following assembly directions.
5 Decorate with ROYAL FROSTING.

HOW TO ENLARGE PATTERNS

Draw crisscross lines, vertically and horizontally, with a ruler, spacing the lines as indicated. Then copy our pattern, one square at a time, using a ruler or compass if necessary. Cut out enlarged pattern and use as directed.

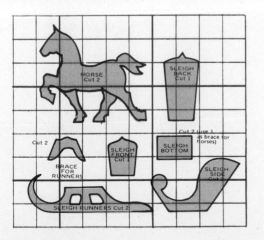

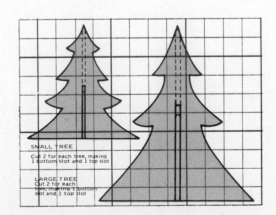

529

Heavenly Cut-Outs
Young artists will be tickled to cut the patterns and help with the decorating.
Bake at 350° for 10 minutes. Makes 6 angels, 12 balls, 6 large stars, and 24 small stars

    3 cups sifted all-purpose flour
      OR: 3 cups instant-type flour
    2 teaspoons baking powder
    ½ teaspoon salt
    ¾ cup (1½ sticks) butter or margarine
    ¾ cup sugar
    1 egg
    ¼ cup dairy sour cream (from an 8-ounce car-
      ton)
    ½ teaspoon vanilla
    ½ teaspoon lemon extract
    1 recipe ORNAMENTAL FROSTING (see index for
      recipe page number)
      Food colorings

1 Sift all-purpose flour, baking powder, and salt into a medium-size bowl. If using instant-type flour, combine, without sifting, with other ingredients.
2 Cream butter or margarine with sugar until fluffy in large bowl; beat in egg, then stir in sour cream and flavorings.
3 Stir in flour mixture, a third at a time, blending well to make a stiff dough. (Instant-type flour gives a crumbly mixture at first, but turns into a smooth dough when kneaded with hands.) Wrap dough in wax paper or transparent wrap; chill several hours, or until firm enough to roll. (Overnight is even better.)
4 Cut patterns for angels, balls, and large and small stars from cardboard, following directions that follow. Or use your own favorite cutters.
5 Cut off about half of dough; keep remaining chilled. Roll out, about ¼ inch thick, on a lightly floured pastry cloth or board. Lay patterns on dough and cut around them with a sharp knife, or cut out with cutters. Lift cut-outs carefully onto ungreased cookie sheets. Roll and cut remaining dough and trimmings the same way.
6 Bake in moderate oven (350°) 10 minutes, or until firm but not brown. Remove from cookie sheets; cool completely on wire racks.
7 Make ORNAMENTAL FROSTING and divide into custard cups. Leave one white; tint remaining

Angels, trees, reindeer, birds, decorated Christmas balls, and twinkling stars, are all crisp cookies.

with your choice of food colorings. Fit writing tip onto a cake-decorating set; fill with frosting, one color at a time, and decorate cookies as pictured or as you wish. Let stand until frosting is firm.

Forest Fantasies
Flavor blend of honey and spice is just right for a youngster's taste. And the dough rolls beautifully.
Bake at 350° for 8 minutes. Makes 24 reindeer, 24 trees, 24 large birds, and 48 small birds

    4 cups sifted all-purpose flour
      OR: 4 cups instant-type flour
    1 tablespoon dry cocoa (not a mix)
    1 teaspoon baking soda
    1 teaspoon pumpkin-pie spice
    ¼ teaspoon salt
    ½ cup (1 stick) butter or margarine
    ¼ cup sugar
    1 egg
    ¾ cup honey
    1 teaspoon grated lemon rind
    1 recipe ORNAMENTAL FROSTING (see index for
      recipe page number)
      Food colorings

1 Sift all-purpose flour, cocoa, baking soda, pumpkin-pie spice, and salt into a medium-size bowl. If using instant-type flour, combine, without sifting, with other ingredients.
2 Cream butter or margarine with sugar until fluffy in a large bowl; beat in egg, honey, and lemon rind.
3 Stir in flour mixture, a third at a time, blending well to make a stiff dough. (Instant-type flour gives a crumbly mixture at first but turns into a smooth dough when kneaded with hands). Wrap dough in wax paper or transparent wrap; chill several hours, or until firm enough to roll. (Overnight is even better.)
4 Cut patterns for trees, birds, and reindeer from cardboard, following directions. Or use your own favorite cutters.
5 Cut off about a quarter of dough; keep remaining chilled. Roll out, ⅛ inch thick, on a lightly floured pastry cloth or board. Lay patterns on dough and cut around them with a sharp knife, or cut out with cutters. Lift cutouts carefully onto greased cookie sheets. Roll and cut remaining dough and trimmings the same way.
6 Bake in moderate oven (350°) 8 minutes, or until firm. Remove carefully from cookie sheets; cool completely on wire racks.
7 Make ORNAMENTAL FROSTING and divide into custard cups. Leave one white; tint remaining with your choice of food colorings. Fit writing

tip onto cake-decorating set; fill with frosting, one color at a time, and decorate cookies as pictured or any way you like. Let stand until frosting is firm.

Marching Soldiers

Sugar cookies, delicately flavored with orange, make these charmers for the kindergarten set.
Bake at 350° for 10 minutes. Makes 15 soldiers

    2 cups sifted all-purpose flour
      OR: 2 cups instant-type flour
    ½ teaspoon baking powder
    ¼ teaspoon salt
    ½ cup (1 stick) butter or margarine
    ⅔ cup sugar
    1 egg
    1 tablespoon frozen concentrated orange juice
      (from a 6-ounce can)
    2 recipes ORNAMENTAL FROSTING (see index for
      recipe page number)
    1 square unsweetened chocolate, melted
      OR: 1 envelope (1 ounce) liquid unsweetened
      chocolate-flavor baking ingredient
    1 tablespoon butter or margarine, melted
    1 teaspoon hot water
      Silver candies
      Food colorings

1 Sift all-purpose flour, baking powder, and salt into a small bowl. If using instant-type flour, combine, without sifting, with other ingredients.
2 Cream butter or margarine with sugar until fluffy in a large bowl; beat in egg and concentrated orange juice.
3 Stir in flour mixture, half at a time, blending well to make a stiff dough. (Instant-type flour gives a crumbly mixture at first but turns into a smooth dough when kneaded with hands.) Wrap dough in wax paper or transparent wrap; chill several hours, or until firm enough to roll. (Overnight is even better.)
4 Cut patterns from cardboard, using directions that follow.
5 Cut off about half of dough; keep remaining chilled. Roll out, ⅛ inch thick, on a lightly floured pastry cloth or board. Lay pattern on dough and cut around it with a sharp knife. Lift cut-outs carefully onto ungreased cookie sheets. Roll and cut out the remaining half of dough and trimmings the same way.
6 Bake in moderate oven (350°) 10 minutes, or until firm but not brown. Remove from cookie sheets; cool completely on wire racks.
7 Make ORNAMENTAL FROSTING. Measure ½ cup

into a small bowl; blend in chocolate, melted butter or margarine, and water. Spread on cookies to make hats, jackets, and shoes as pictured; press silver candies into frosting for buttons on jackets.
8 Divide remaining frosting into custard cups. Leave one white; tint remaining with your choice of food colorings. Fit writing tip onto a cake-decorating set; fill with frosting, 1 color at a time, and finish decorating cookies as pictured. Let stand until frosting is firm.

Toyland Cut-Outs

Let little tots pick their favorites, then lend a hand in cutting and decorating.

Bake at 350° for 8 minutes. Makes about 8 dozen tiny and 8 dozen cookies

    3½ cups sifted all-purpose flour
    3½ teaspoons baking powder
    ½ teaspoon salt
    ⅓ cup butter or margarine
    ⅓ cup firmly packed brown sugar
    ⅔ cup honey
    1 egg
    1 teaspoon lemon extract
    1 recipe ORNAMENTAL FROSTING (see index for
      recipe page number)

1 Measure dry ingredients into sifter.
2 Cream butter or margarine with brown sugar until light in medium-size bowl; beat in honey, egg, and lemon extract.
3 Sift in dry ingredients, blending well. (Dough will be stiff.) Chill overnight, or until firm enough to roll.
4 Roll out, a small amount at a time, to ⅛-inch thickness on floured pastry cloth or board. Cut out cookies with floured cutters, or cut around your own cardboard pattern with a sharp knife. Place on greased cookie sheets.
5 Bake in moderate oven (350°) 8 minutes, or until firm but not browned. Remove from cookie sheets; cool completely on wire racks. Decorate with tinted ORNAMENTAL FROSTING, letting your imagination guide you.

Paper-Doll Cookies

Busy little cooks will delight in decorating these doll-size charmers.
Bake at 350° about 10 minutes. Makes 6 doll cookies and 6 dresses

    1 cup (2 sticks) butter or margarine
    1 cup sugar
    2 eggs
    1 teaspoon vanilla

3 cups sifted all-purpose flour
½ teaspoon salt
1 recipe PAPER-DOLL FROSTING *(recipe follows)*
Red, green, blue, and yellow food colorings
Cinnamon and silver candies
Multicolor sprinkles

1 Cream butter or margarine until soft in medium-size bowl; gradually add sugar, creaming
after each addition, until light and fluffy.
2 Beat in eggs and vanilla; sift in flour and salt;
blend well to make a stiff dough; chill 2 to 3
hours, or until firm enough to roll easily.
3 Roll out chilled dough, ¼ of recipe at a time,
to ⅛-inch thickness on floured small cookie
sheet (keep unused dough chilled); cut around
paper-doll patterns (cut from child's paper-doll

CHRISTMAS COOKIE PATTERNS—First rule off
squares on a sheet of paper, allowing 1″ for each
square needed. Locate and mark points on each
square where the design you want cuts through. Con-
nect the points, following the outline below, and cut
out the pattern.

533

book) with tip of sharp knife to make 2 dolls; remove dough trimmings; repeat to make 6 dolls in all.

4 Roll out remaining dough and trimmings to ⅛-inch thickness on floured pastry cloth or board; cut around paper-doll dresses in the same way to make 6 dresses; transfer with pancake turner to ungreased cookie sheet.

5 Bake in moderate oven (350°) 10 minutes, or until golden-brown; cool slightly, then carefully remove with pancake turner; cool completely on wire cake racks before decorating.

6 Divide PAPER-DOLL FROSTING among five custard cups; leave one plain; tint remaining with food colorings; decorate dolls and dresses with frosting put through cake decorating set and with sprinkles and candies, following designs on patterns cut from book or any way you wish; spread underside of dress cookie with frosting; place on doll cookie; let set to harden.

●

Paper-Doll Frosting
Makes about 1 cup

2 egg whites
¼ teaspoon cream of tartar
¼ teaspoon vanilla
2½ cups sifted 10X (confectioners' powdered) sugar

Beat egg whites, cream of tartar, and vanilla until foamy: gradually beat in sugar until frosting stands in firm peaks.

GROWN-UP RECIPES FOR CHILDREN TO TRY

Satellite Eggs
Makes 1 serving

1 teaspoon butter or bacon fat
1 egg

1 Use a small frying pan that's about 5 inches across.
2 Heat the pan *slowly* with 1 teaspoon butter or bacon fat.
3 Break the egg into a cup—don't let the yolk break—then slide it into the pan.
4 Cook it slowly. It shouldn't sputter. If it does, you're frying it too fast.
5 When the white part begins to set, make a ring of thin frankfurter slices on it, all around the yolk.
6 Now finish cooking the egg—still slowly—the way you like it.

Wolf-Patrol Flapjacks
Pile 'em, five cakes high, with butter between. Top with cart-wheel spokes of assorted-flavor jams. Raid the refrigerator for milk to drink. Makes 5 big cakes

1 cup pancake mix
1 cup milk
1 egg
1 tablespoon vegetable oil
Soft butter for spreading
jams for spreading (strawberry, blackberry, cherry, apricot)

1 Pour milk into a big jar with cover.
2 Add pancake mix, egg, vegetable oil.
3 Screw cover down tight.
4 Shake hard 10 times. Take off cover.
5 Flip a few drops of water on heated griddle. They'll dance around when heat's just right.
6 Grease griddle by placing pat of butter in center and tilting griddle so butter melts evenly over it; pour on batter; bake until you see lots of holes on top; flip; bake other side.

●

PARTY PASTRIES
Three dainty sweets come from just one package of vanilla—or chocolate-flavor instant-pudding mix. Make the pudding following the instructions on the package. *Then:*

For Make Believe Napoleons
Graham crackers
1 teaspoon milk
¼ cup 10X (confectioners' powdered) sugar
2 tablespoons semisweet-chocolate pieces

1 Halve graham crackers. Spread with pudding; make 3 layers.
2 Top each with a halved cracker spread with icing made by stirring 1 teaspoon milk into ¼ cup 10X (confectioners' powdered) sugar.
3 Melt 2 tablespoons semisweet-chocolate pieces in a tiny pan over hot water.
4 Make stripes across tops with small knife dipped into melted chocolate. Run knife lengthwise across stripes to make design.

For Mock Eclairs
Ladyfingers
Semisweet-chocolate pieces
Whipped-cream-in-a-can

1 Make "sandwiches" of pudding and ladyfingers.
2 Frost with icing made by melting semisweet-chocolate pieces over hot water.
3 Pipe cream around edge with whipped-cream-in-a-can.

534

Beginnings of a grown-up meal: rosy Cranberry Fizz, Creamy Shrimp Dip Tray and Stuffed Baked Potatoes.

For Pudding Horns

Sugar Ice-cream cones
Whipped-cream-in-a-can

1 Fill sugar ice-cream cones with pudding.
2 Trim edge with whipped-cream-in-a-can.

A GROWN-UP MEAL CHILDREN CAN MAKE

Cranberry Fizz
Creamy Shrimp Dip Tray
(served in living room)
Rolled Roast of Beef
Stuffed Baked Potatoes
Tomato-Lima Cups
Parker House Cheesies
Candy Blossom Cake
Coffee   Milk

To help children off to a good start, suggest a look at the pictures on these pages. Color photos show the finished foods; the others, how special steps are done.

Cranberry Fizz, for example, is trimmed with fancy-edge lemon slices. Our young cook is shown making these at the top of the page by cutting out tiny V-shape pieces all around the edge of each slice.

Creamy Shrimp Dip, served with the punch and next to it in the color photo, is so easy that no how-to photo is needed.

Rolled Roast of Beef and *Stuffed Baked Potatoes* are served together, so that's how we'll talk about them. After potatoes are baked, the insides are scooped out, mashed, and put back in the shells. Our cook shows how to handle a hot potato—with a pot holder for protection. The big beautiful roast is actually simplest of all—just leave it in the oven till it's done. Best way to be sure: Use a meat thermometer. Push it, bulb end down, through top of roast into center.

Tomato-Lima Cup salads call for peeled tomatoes—a cinch when you dip each one in a pan of hot water, hold it there about a minute. Skin will peel right off.

Parker House Cheesies are another snap: Ready-baked rolls with cheese triangles tucked in folds, heated for 10 minutes.

Candy Blossom Cake sprouts marshmallow flowers. To make, cut marshmallows in half, snip around edge of each half with scissors, put piece of gumdrop in center. For a neat, pretty frosting job, do the side first, moving spatula up and down instead of sideways, then frost top.

●

Your Shopping List

Roast beef (one 4 to 5-pound rolled boned rib roast)
Shrimps (one 5-ounce can)
Dairy sour cream (one 8-ounce carton)
Sliced American cheese (one 8-ounce package)
Baking potatoes (6 large)
Fresh tomatoes (6 medium)
Water cress (1 bunch)
Lettuce (1 head)
Parsley (1 bunch)
Frozen baby lima beans (one 10-ounce package)
Ready-baked Parker House rolls (1 dozen)
Corn chips (1 package, to go with dip)
Favorite crackers (1 box), to go with dip)
Yellow cake mix (1 package)
Fluffy white frosting mix (2 packages)

535

536

Worthy of the best French chef, lordly Rolled Roast.

To round out a grown-up meal: cool Tomato-Lima Cups, Parker House Cheesies, Candy Blossom Cake.

Cranberry-juice cocktail (one 16-ounce bottle)
Imitation citrus-flavor carbonated beverage (one 10-ounce bottle)
Green-onion dip mix (1 envelope)
Flavored marshmallows, tiny gumdrops, and leaf-shape jelly candies (enough to decorate cake)

Probably in the Refrigerator or Cupboard

Mayonnaise or salad dressing
Butter or margarine
Milk
Eggs
Catsup
Horseradish
Lemons
Salt and pepper
Vegetable oil
Vinegar
Sugar
Paprika
Almond extract
Yellow food coloring
Maraschino cherries
Toasted slivered almonds
Stuffed green olives
Pitted ripe olives
Pimiento

Your Suggested Work Plan

The day before:
1 Put bottles of cranberry juice and carbonated beverage in refrigerator.
2 Mix shrimp dip; cover dish; chill.
3 Peel tomatoes; place on a plate; cover and chill.
4 Cook lima beans; toss with dressing; cover dish and chill.
5 Bake cake layers; cool and wrap. Chop maraschino cherries for filling; set aside in covered dish. Make marshmallow flowers; wrap in transparent wrap so they won't dry out. All of these foods can be left on counter top or go on a shelf, as Mother prefers.

6 Scrub and dry potatoes; leave on counter top. Wash lettuce and water cress; dry well on paper toweling; place in vegetable crisper in refrigerator.

The morning of the dinner:
1 Make cake filling and frosting; put layers together and decorate completely.
2 Get cheese rolls ready for baking; place on cookie sheet. Wrap in transparent wrap and set aside until time to heat (10 minutes before serving time).
3 Make olive-pimiento decorations for tomato salads and cut lemon slices for punch. Wrap separately (plastic bags are good) and put in refrigerator.

Starting about 3 hours before dinner:
1 Season roast and put in oven.
2 When meat has been in about an hour, place potatoes in with it.
3 Set the table.
4 Scoop out insides of tomatoes and fill with lima beans; lay lettuce leaves on salad plates and top each with a tomato cup. Refrigerate until serving time.
5 Make coffee.
6 Take potatoes out of oven when done; scoop and refill them; put back in oven to reheat.
7 Spoon shrimp dip into serving bowl; arrange on tray with corn chips and crackers.
8 Remove roast from oven and place on serving platter; cover with foil and let stand (makes slicing easier).
9 Mix cranberry punch; take pitcher, glasses, and shrimp tray into living room to serve.
10 Place rolls in oven to heat.
11 Remove potatoes and rolls from oven; place on serving plates.
12 Garnish salads; place on table; bring roast beef to table.
13 Clear table; serve cake and coffee.

Cranberry Fizz
Makes 6 servings

1 bottle (16 ounces) cranberry-juice cocktail, chilled
1 bottle (10 ounces) low-calorie imitation citrus-flavor carbonated beverage, chilled
1 lemon, cut in 6 slices

1 Just before serving, mix cranberry-juice

cocktail and carbonated beverage in a large pitcher; pour into 6 small glasses.

2 Make a slit in each lemon slice from outside edge to center; hang over edge of each glass. (To make notched slices as pictured, cut small V-shape pieces all the way around from rind of each slice with a small sharp-tip knife.)

•

Creamy Shrimp Dip Tray
Makes 6 servings

    1 can (about 5 ounces) deveined shrimps
    ½ cup mayonnaise or salad dressing
    ½ cup dairy sour cream
    ¼ cup catsup
    1 teaspoon lemon juice
    1 teaspoon prepared horseradish
        Corn chips
        Crackers

1 Empty shrimps into a sieve and rinse under cold water. Set aside 1 shrimp for garnish; cut remainder into small pieces.

2 Combine mayonnaise or salad dressing, sour cream, catsup, lemon juice, and horseradish in a medium-size bowl; fold in shrimps. Chill at least two hours or overnight to blend flavors.

3 Spoon into a small bowl. Garnish with saved shrimp and a tiny sprig of parsley, if you wish. Serve with corn chips and crisp crackers.

Rolled Roast of Beef
Roast at 325° for 2 to 2½ hours. Makes 6 servings plus enough for one bonus meal

    1 rolled boned rib roast of beef, weighing 4 to
        5 pounds
    2 teaspoons salt
        Watercress

1 Preheat oven to slow (325°).

2 Wipe roast with damp paper toweling. Sprinkle meat all over with salt, then place, fat side up, on a rack in an open roasting pan. Stick meat thermometer into roast so the bulb end reaches the center of the meat. Do not add water or cover pan. Place in oven.

3 Roast in slow oven (325°) 2 to 2½ hours, or until thermometer registers 140° for rare or 160° for medium.

4 Remove meat from oven and place on a serv-

ing platter; cover loosely with foil and let stand about 20 minutes. (This makes roast easier to slice.)

5 Cut 2 or 3 strings away from meat, then trim a thin slice from the bottom so roast will stand upright on platter. Place sprigs of watercress around meat.

•

Stuffed Baked Potatoes
Bake at 325° for 1¾ hours. Makes 6 servings

    6 large baking potatoes
        Vegetable oil
    ¾ cup milk
    4 tablespoons (½ stick) butter or margarine
    1 envelope (2 packets) green-onion dip mix

1 Scrub potatoes with a vegetable brush; dry with paper toweling. Rub skins all over with vegetable oil to keep them soft. Place potatoes in a large shallow pan.

2 Bake in same slow oven (325°) with roast, 1½ hours, or until potatoes are soft; remove from oven but leave heat turned on.

3 Using pot holders to protect your fingers, cut a slice lengthwise from top of each potato and lift off. Carefully scoop out the insides with a teaspoon and place in a large bowl. (Be careful not to break shells.) Return shells to pan.

4 Combine milk, butter or margarine, and onion dip mix in a small saucepan; heat slowly until butter melts.

5 Mash potatoes in bowl; beat in hot milk mixture until potatoes are fluffy. Spoon back into shells, mounding slightly. Return to oven.

6 Bake 15 minutes longer, or until lightly browned on top. Arrange potatoes on a serving platter. If you wish, sprinkle potatoes with sliced fresh green onions, pressing slices down lightly into potatoes, and use the green tops to trim the platter.

539

Tomato-Lima Cups
Makes 6 servings

    1 package (10 ounces) frozen baby lima beans
    ¾ teaspoon salt
    ½ teaspoon sugar
    ¼ teaspoon paprika
    ⅛ teaspoon pepper
    ½ cup chopped parsley
    ⅓ cup vegetable oil
    3 tablespoons cider vinegar

6 medium-size firm ripe tomatoes, washed
   Lettuce
6 stuffed green olives
3 small pitted ripe olives, halved crosswise
1 pimiento, cut in 6 strips

1 Cook lima beans, following label directions; drain well; place in a medium-size bowl.
2 Measure salt, sugar, paprika, pepper, parsley, vegetable oil, and vinegar into beans; toss until well-mixed and beans are shiny. Cover with transparent wrap and chill several hours or overnight.
3 Heat a pan of water just until bubbly. Holding tomatoes, one at a time, on a slotted spoon, dip into water and hold about a minute, then lift out and place in a pie plate to cool. Cut a thin slice from the top of each tomato, then peel off skin. Scoop out the insides with a teaspoon, being careful not to break shells. Turn tomatoes upside down in plate to drain; cover and chill.
4 One or two hours before serving, place a large lettuce leaf on each of 6 salad plates; stand a tomato cup on each leaf; spoon lima bean mixture into cups.
5 Slide a green olive onto each of 6 wooden picks, then a piece of ripe olive and a strip of pimiento. Stand one pick in center of each tomato cup. Chill until serving time.

Candy Blossom Cake
Bake at 350° for 30 minutes. Makes 1 nine-inch layer cake

1 package yellow cake mix
   Eggs
   Water
2 packages fluffy white frosting mix
   Boiling water
⅓ cup toasted slivered almonds (from a 5-ounce can)
⅓ cup chopped maraschino cherries
½ teaspoon almond extract
   Yellow food coloring
10 flavored marshmallows (from a 10-ounce package)
   Tiny colored gumdrops and leaf-shape jelly candies

1 Preheat oven to moderate (350°).
2 Grease bottoms of 2 nine-inch layer-cake pans; line with wax paper; grease paper.
3 Prepare cake mix with eggs and water, following label directions; pour into prepared cake pans, dividing evenly.

4 Bake in moderate oven (350°) 30 minutes, or until tops spring back when lightly pressed with fingertip. Cool in pans on wire racks 5 minutes. Run the tip of a small knife around inside edges of pans to loosen layers; invert onto racks; peel off wax paper; cool layers completely.
5 Prepare both packages of frosting mix with boiling water, following label directions. Measure 1 cup of the frosting into another small bowl and stir in almonds, cherries, and almond extract. Set aside. (This will be cake filling.)
6 Stir a few drops yellow food coloring into remaining frosting to tint pale yellow.
7 Brush around edges of cake layers with a pastry brush to remove any loose crumbs. Place one layer, top side down, on a serving plate. Spread with almond-cherry filling, spreading not quite to edge; place second layer, flat side down, on top. Spread yellow frosting around side and top of cake, piling any extra frosting in center of top to hold candy flowers.
8 To make flowers, cut each marshmallow in half crosswise with scissors. (To keep scissors from sticking, dip blades in 10X [confectioners' powdered] sugar, tapping off any extra.) Holding each piece of marshmallow, flat side down, snip 6 times around edge, cutting from outside almost to center.
9 Cut tops off 20 gumdrops with a small knife; place one in the center of each marshmallow flower. Arrange on top of cake. Place leaf-shape candies around flowers.

Parker House Cheesies
Bake at 325° for 10 minutes. Makes 6 servings

12 ready-baked Parker House rolls
 3 slices process American cheese (from an 8-ounce package)

1 Separate rolls, then pull each apart slightly at the fold.
2 Cut each slice of cheese in half lengthwise, then in half crosswise; cut each piece into 2 small triangles. Tuck 2 triangles, one on top of the other, in each roll; press edges together. Place rolls on a cookie sheet.
3 Heat in slow oven (325°) 10 minutes, or until cheese starts to melt.

An alternate finale for the grown-up meal might be an exquisite tray of fresh fruits and aged cheeses.

COLD WEATHER

WARMERS

**COLD WEATHER WARMERS:
HEARTY, HOT RECIPES
TO WARM BODY AND SOUL**

Nothing warms a wintry day faster than homey, hearty main dishes: juicy meat pies, for example, blanketed with crisply golden crusts, touched here and there with brown; simple savory casseroles served bubbling, straight from the oven; hot sizzling sandwiches, the bigger the better. There's a coziness about such dishes, a remembrance of things past when kitchens were warm and welcoming, when children, red-cheeked from an afternoon of sledding or snowman-building, lined up their boots on the stoop, then dashed stocking-footed for the warmth of a fire, crackling on the hearth. Appetites were ravenous, suppers robust, with plenty of seconds and thirds for all.

Collected here are some up-to-date versions of such old-fashioned winter favorites, plus a selection of meals-in-themselves hot sandwiches. They're easy to make, guaranteed to warm both the heart and the hands.

543

Sure-fire way to warm up the family when the wind and snow are swooshing 'round the eaves: Continental Veal Pie, a savory, bubbly medley of peppery Italian sausages, chunks of veal shoulder, onions, carrots and zucchini. Magic ingredient? A spaghetti sauce mix.

HEARTY MAIN DISHES

Continental Veal Pie

Spaghetti-sauce mix and hot sausages give this hearty veal dish an old-world flavor.
Bake at 425° for 30 minutes. Makes 6 servings

    1½ pounds veal shoulder, cut in 1-inch cubes
      3 tablespoons all-purpose flour
      3 tablespoons olive oil or vegetable oil
      2 Italian hot sausages, sliced ½-inch thick
     12 small white onions, peeled
      1 envelope (2¼ ounces) spaghetti-sauce mix
        with tomato
      3 cups water
     12 small carrots, pared and cut in sticks
      6 medium-size zucchini, trimmed and cut in
        sticks
     ¼ pound fresh mushrooms, sliced
        OR: 1 can (3 or 4 ounces) sliced
        mushrooms
      1 package piecrust mix
      1 egg
      1 tablespoon milk
        Few drops liquid red pepper seasoning

1 Shake veal, a few pieces at a time, with flour in paper bag to coat evenly. Brown quickly in olive oil or vegetable oil in large heavy kettle or Dutch oven; push to one side.
2 Brown sausages in same kettle; push to one side; add onions and brown lightly.
3 Combine spaghetti-sauce mix and water in 4-cup measure. (Mix has tomato right in it, so all you need to add is the water.) Stir into kettle; cover. Simmer 1½ hours, or until veal is tender.
4 Cook carrots and zucchini sticks together in boiling salted water in large saucepan 15 minutes, or just until tender; drain well.
5 Mound veal mixture, cooked vegetables, and mushrooms into a round 8-cup baking dish.
6 Prepare piecrust mix, following label directions, or make pastry from your own favorite one-crust recipe. Roll out on lightly floured pastry cloth or board to a circle 3 inches larger than baking dish; cut a 4-inch cross in center. Fold points of cross back so gravy won't darken pastry; lay circle over rolling pin and transfer to baking dish. Trim overhang to 1 inch; fold under flush with rim; flute.

7 Roll out all trimmings ¼-inch thick; cut into fancy shapes with truffle or small cookie cutters.
8 Beat egg slightly with milk and red-pepper seasoning in a cup; brush part over pie. Place cut-outs around edge; brush them also. Cover

center hole with a small piece of foil to keep vegetables from drying out during baking.
9 Bake in hot oven (425°) 15 minutes; brush again with egg mixture. Bake 15 minutes longer, or until golden. Cut in wedges.

●

Crisscross Chicken Pie

A combination of the old and the new with big chunks of chicken in a curry-sparked sauce.
Bake at 400° for 20 minutes, then at 350° for 25 minutes. Makes 6 servings

      1 broiler-fryer, cut up (3 pounds)
      3 cups water
        Handful of celery tops
      1 teaspoon salt (for chicken)
      6 peppercorns
        CURRY-CREAM SAUCE (recipe follows)
      1 package (10 ounces) frozen peas, cooked
        and drained
      1 pimiento, chopped
      2 cups sifted all-purpose flour
      1 teaspoon salt (for pastry)
     ⅓ cup vegetable shortening
     ⅔ cup milk

1 Simmer chicken with water, celery tops, 1 teaspoon salt, and peppercorns in kettle 1 hour, or until tender. Remove from broth and let cool until easy to handle.
2 Strain broth into 4-cup measure; add water, if needed, to make 3 cups. Make CURRY-CREAM SAUCE.
3 Slip skin from chicken, then remove meat from bones. (It comes off easily while still warm.) Cut into bite-size pieces; toss with peas, pimiento, and 2 cups of CURRY-CREAM SAUCE in medium-size bowl. Set aside for Step 5. (Save remaining sauce to reheat and serve over pie.)
4 Sift flour and 1 teaspoon salt into medium-size bowl; cut in shortening with pastry blender until mixture is crumbly; stir in milk with a fork just until dough holds together.
5 Turn out onto lightly floured pastry cloth or board; knead lightly 5 or 6 times. Roll out ⅔ of dough to a rectangle, 16x12; fit into a baking dish, 10x6x2. Spoon filling into shell.
6 Roll out remaining pastry to a rectangle about 14x7; cut into 9 long strips, each about ¾ inch wide, with knife or pastry wheel. Lay 5 strips lengthwise over filling. Halve remaining 4 strips; weave across long strips to make a crisscross top. Trim overhang to 1 inch; fold under; flute.
7 Bake in hot oven (400°) 20 minutes; reduce heat to moderate (350°). Bake 25 minutes longer, or until golden. Cut into 6 servings. Serve with remaining hot CURRY-CREAM SAUCE.
    CURRY-CREAM SAUCE—Melt 6 tablespoons (¾ stick) butter or margarine over low heat in me-

Olive-studded Tuna-Cheese Imperial. To top: an hourglass of soft bread crumbs.

dium-size saucepan. Stir in 6 tablespoons all-purpose flour, 1 teaspoon salt, 1 teaspoon curry powder, and ⅛ teaspoon pepper. Cook, stirring all the time, just until mixture bubbles. Stir in 3 cups chicken broth slowly; continue cooking and stirring until sauce thickens and boils 1 minute. Stir in 1 tall can (14½ ounces) evaporated milk. Makes about 4½ cups.

●

Tuna-Cheese Imperial
Bake at 350° for 30 minutes. Makes 6 servings

   1 package (8 ounces) wide noodles
   ½ cup (1 stick) butter or margarine
   5 tablespoons all-purpose flour
   1 teaspoon salt
  ¼ teaspoon pepper
2½ cups milk
   1 package (8 ounces) cream cheese
   1 can (about 7 ounces) tuna, drained
   ½ cup sliced pimiento-stuffed olives

   2 tablespoons cut chives
   1 package (6 ounces) sliced Muenster cheese
1½ cups soft bread crumbs (3 slices)

1 Cook noodles, following label directions; drain.
2 Melt 5 tablespoons of the butter or margarine in a medium-size saucepan; stir in flour, salt, and pepper; cook, stirring constantly, until bubbly. Stir in milk; continue cooking and stirring until sauce thickens and boils 1 minute. Slice cream cheese into sauce; stir until melted, then stir in tuna, olives, and chives; remove from heat.
3 Pour about ¾ cup of the sauce into a greased 10-cup baking dish, then layer other ingredients on top this way: Half of the noodles, half of remaining sauce, 2 slices Muenster cheese, remaining noodles, half of remaining sauce, remaining Muenster cheese, and remaining sauce.
4 Melt remaining 3 tablespoons butter or mar-

545

Super, supper platter: Garden-Pepper Pie (in the center) ringed with a spiral of Spicy Glazed Pork Chops.

garine in a small saucepan; add bread crumbs; toss lightly with a fork. Sprinkle over mixture in baking dish or place in a pattern as pictured.
5 Bake in moderate oven (350°) 30 minutes, or until bubbly.

●

Baked Tuna Dinner
Bake at 350° for 30 minutes. Makes 8 servings

½ cup uncooked regular rice
1 envelope instant vegetable broth
  OR: 1 vegetable-bouillon cube
  Water
1 package (10 ounces) frozen peas
2 cans (about 7 ounces each) tuna, drained and flaked
½ cup chopped celery
2 tablespoons chopped parsley
1 can (10½ ounces) condensed golden mushroom soup
½ cup milk
¼ teaspoon leaf basil, crumbled
¼ teaspoon pepper
3 hard-cooked eggs, shelled and sliced
4 tablespoons (½ stick) butter or margarine
1½ cups crushed cheese crackers

1 Cook rice with vegetable broth and water, following label directions. Spoon into an 8-cup baking dish.
2 Cook peas, following label directions; drain. Add to rice with tuna, celery, and parsley.
3 Blend soup, milk, basil, and pepper in a small bowl; pour over tuna mixture; toss lightly to mix. Place egg slices in a layer on top.
4 Melt butter or margarine in a small saucepan; remove from heat. Stir in crackers until moist; sprinkle over eggs in baking dish.
5 Bake in moderate oven (350°) 30 minutes, or until bubbly.

●

Cottage-Cheese Strata
Bake at 350° for 1 hour. Makes 6 servings

4 eggs
1½ cups milk
1 can (10½ ounces) condensed cream of potato soup
6 tablespoons (¾ stick) butter or margarine, melted
12 slices white bread
1 carton (1 pound) cream-style cottage cheese.
½ cup grated Romano cheese
1 tablespoon instant minced onion
1 teaspoon salt
1 teaspoon dillweed
1 can (1 pound) cut green beans, drained

1 Beat eggs well in a large bowl; stir in milk, soup, and melted butter or margarine. Pour 1 cupful into a baking dish, 13x9x2.
2 Place 6 slices of the bread in dish; drizzle another 1 cup egg mixture over bread.
3 Mix cottage cheese, ¼ cup of the Romano cheese, onion, salt, and dillweed in a medium-size bowl; spoon evenly over bread; top with green beans. Cover beans with remaining 6 slices bread; drizzle remaining egg mixture over top, then sprinkle with remaining Romano cheese.
4 Bake in moderate oven (350°) 1 hour, or until puffed and lightly golden. Let stand about 15 minutes before serving.

Spicy Glazed Pork Chops with Apricots
Syrup from apricots gives chops and fruit a shiny coat and tart-sweet flavor.
Bake at 400° for 1 hour and 15 minutes. Makes 6 servings

1 can (1 pound, 14 ounces) whole apricots
1 tablespoon bottled steak sauce
1 teaspoon salt
6 rib or loin pork chops, cut ½ inch thick
1 teaspoon whole cloves

1 Drain syrup from apricots into medium-size saucepan; stir in steak sauce and salt. Heat to boiling; cook, uncovered, 15 minutes, or until syrup thickens slightly. (Save apricots for Step 3.)
2 Brush chops on both sides with half of syrup; arrange in single layer in shallow baking pan. Do not cover.
3 Bake in hot oven (400°) 45 minutes; turn chops. Stud apricots with cloves; arrange around chops; brush all with remaining syrup.
4 Bake 30 minutes longer, or until chops are tender and richly glazed.

●

Garden Pepper Pie
Golden cornmeal crust holds a creamy custard filling dotted with crisp pepper squares.
Bake at 400° for 30 minutes. Makes 6 servings

Crust
¾ cup sifted all-purpose flour
½ cup yellow cornmeal
1½ teaspoons baking powder
½ teaspoon salt
4 tablespoons vegetable shortening
⅓ cup milk

Filling

2 medium-size sweet red peppers
2 medium-size green peppers
1 large onion, chopped (1 cup)
4 tablespoons (½ stick) butter or margarine
3 tablespoons all-purpose flour
1 teaspoon salt
1 teaspoon leaf oregano, crumbled
1 egg
¾ cup milk

1 Make crust. Combine flour, cornmeal, baking powder, and salt in medium-size bowl; cut in shortening with pastry blender until mixture is crumbly. Stir in milk with a fork just until dough clings together and leaves side of bowl clean.
2 Press evenly over bottom and side of a 10-inch pie plate or 6-cup shallow baking dish.
3 Make filling: Wash peppers; cut out stems, seeds, and membrane; cut peppers into 1-inch squares. Parboil in small amount boiling salted water in medium-size saucepan 5 minutes; drain.
4 Sauté onion in butter or margarine in same saucepan; stir in drained peppers. Sprinkle with flour, salt, and oregano; toss lightly to mix; spoon into shell.
5 Beat eggs slightly with milk in 2-cup measure; pour over vegetables.
6 Bake in hot oven (400°) 30 minutes, or until top is golden and custard is set but still soft in center. Let stand 10 to 15 minutes; cut into wedges.

Potato Pancakes

So traditional with pot roast—and all the better topped with savory-rich gravy.
Makes 6 servings

548

4 medium-size potatoes
1 small onion
2 eggs
1 teaspoon salt
¼ teaspoon pepper
  Vegetable shortening, bacon drippings, or vegetable oil for frying

1 Pare and coarsely shred potatoes onto wax papar, then measure. (There should be 2 cups.) Place in bowl.
2 Grate in onion; stir in eggs, salt, and pepper just until blended.
3 Heat enough shortening, bacon drippings, or vegetable oil to make ⅛-inch depth in large frying pan.
4 Spoon batter, a scant ¼ cupful for each pancake, into hot fat, spreading to make a very thin cake. Cook slowly, turning once, 3 to 5 minutes on each side, or until crisp and golden. Drain on paper toweling.

Tomato-Kraut Cups

Scooped-out tomatoes are filled brimful with tangy seasoned sauerkraut.
Makes 6 servings

1 can (about 1 pound) sauerkraut
6 medium-size firm ripe tomatoes
3 tablespoons vegetable oil
1 tablespoon cider vinegar
1 tablespoon catsup
1 small onion, grated
1 teaspoon sugar
⅛ teaspoon salt
½ teaspoon Worcestershire sauce
  Shredded lettuce

1 Drain sauerkraut; pat dry between sheets of paper toweling. Chop coarsely and place in large bowl.
2 Wash tomatoes and cut off tops; scoop out insides with teaspoon. Turn tomato cups upside down to drain, then chill. Chop tomato pulp; add to sauerkraut.
3 Combine vegetable oil, vinegar, catsup, onion, sugar, salt, and Worcestershire sauce in a cup; pour over sauerkraut mixture; toss lightly to mix. Let stand 30 minutes to blend flavors.
4 When ready to serve, heap sauerkraut mixture in tomato cups; place on individual serving plates lined with shredded lettuce.

Autumn's Best Pot Roast

Fresh tomato, carrots, and onion season this beef favorite most invitingly.
Makes 6 servings

4 pounds boneless beef chuck pot roast
2 large carrots, pared and grated
1 large tomato, cut up
1 large onion, cut up
1 bay leaf
2 teaspoons salt
4 peppercorns
1 cup water
2 tablespoons all-purpose flour

1 Brown beef in its own fat in large heavy kettle or Dutch oven. Add carrots, tomato, onion, seasonings, and water; cover tight.
2 Simmer 2 to 2½ hours, or until beef is tender. Remove to heated serving platter; keep hot while making gravy.
3 Strain liquid into a 4-cup measure, pressing vegetables through sieve. Let stand about a minute, or until fat rises to top. Skim off fat and return 2 tablespoons to kettle; blend in flour. Add water to liquid, if needed, to make 2 cups; stir into flour mixture. Cook, stirring constantly, until gravy thickens and boils 1 minute.

Tomato-Crown Meat Loaf
Juicy tomato slices give this flavorful moist loaf its rosy topper.
Bake at 350° for 1 hour. Makes 6 servings

   2 *pounds meat-loaf combination (ground beef and pork)*
   1 *cup regular rolled oats*
   1 *small can evaporated milk (⅔ cup)*
   1 *egg*
   1 *small onion, finely chopped (¼ cup)*
   ½ *cup chopped parsley*
   2 *teaspoons salt*
   1 *teaspoon coriander seeds, crushed*
   ⅛ *teaspoon pepper*
   2 *large tomatoes, sliced ¼ inch thick*
   1 *teaspoon sugar*
     Salt and pepper
   2 *tablespoons butter or margarine*

1 Combine meats, rolled oats, evaporated milk, egg, onion, parsley, salt, coriander, and pepper in large bowl; mix lightly with fork.
2 Shape into a flat loaf, about 6 inches square, in middle of shallow baking pan.
3 Bake in moderate oven (350°) 30 minutes. Arrange tomato slices, overlapping, on top; sprinkle with sugar, salt, and pepper; dot with butter or margarine. Bake 30 minutes longer, or until meat is well-done.
4 Remove to heated serving platter; cut in thick slices through tomatoes.

Mashed-Potato Surprise
Pungent flavor of turnip accents the mildness of potato in this fix-easy vegetable dish.
Makes 6 servings

   6 *medium-size potatoes, pared and quartered*
   6 *medium-size white turnips, pared and quartered*
   4 *tablespoons (½ stick) butter or margarine*
   ⅓ *cup milk*
   ½ *teaspoon salt*
   ⅛ *teaspoon pepper*
     Paprika

1 Cook potatoes and turnips together in small amount boiling lightly salted water in medium-size saucepan, 20 minutes, or until tender. Drain and mash, or put through a ricer.
2 Beat in butter or margarine, milk, salt, and pepper until mixture is fluffy.
3 Pile into heated serving dish; top with a dollop of butter or margarine, if you wish; sprinkle with paprika.

Eggplant Scallop
Two of fall's best—eggplant and tomatoes—take on a mellow herb flavor in this top-range vegetable "casserole."
Makes 6 servings

   1 *large onion, chopped (1 cup)*
   1 *teaspoon curry powder*
   2 *tablespoons vegetable oil*
   2 *tablespoons sugar*
   2 *teaspoons mixed Italian herbs*
   2 *teaspoons salt*
   1 *envelope instant beef bouillon*
     OR: 1 beef-bouillon cube
   1 *tablespoon cider vinegar*
   1 *teaspoon Worcestershire sauce*
   ¼ *cup water*
   ½ *cup pitted sliced ripe olives*
   1 *large eggplant, diced (about 8 cups)*
   4 *large ripe tomatoes, diced*
   2 *cups sliced celery*

1 Sauté onion with curry powder in salad oil just until onion is soft in large frying pan; remove from heat.
2 Stir in seasonings, then remaining ingredients; cover.
3 Heat to boiling, then simmer, stirring once or twice, 15 minutes. Uncover; simmer 10 minutes longer, or until eggplant and celery are tender.

549

New way to serve scrambled eggs—riding aboard a chunky, toasted club sandwich.

HEARTY HOT SANDWICHES

Pick your favorite rolls and breads, stack them high with fillings, and you can be sure of putting a hot, wholesome meal on the table fast as days seem to get busier and colder. The filling suggestions here include lots of meat, cheese, and crisp extras—and even the spreads and toppers are built right in.

Tuna Hobos
Bits of mild cheese melt through the tuna-salad filling as each bun bakes in foil.
Bake at 400° for 20 minutes. Makes 4 servings

    1 can (about 7 ounces) tuna, drained and
      flaked
    ¼ cup diced celery
    4 triangles (1 ounce each) process Gruyére
      cheese diced (from a 6- ounce package)
    1 pimiento, diced
    ¼ cup mayonnaise or salad dressing
    1 teaspoon lemon juice
    ½ teaspoon salt
    ½ teaspoon Worcestershire sauce
    4 split hamburger buns, buttered

1 Combine tuna, celery, cheese, parsley, and pimiento in a medium-size bowl.
2 Blend mayonnaise or salad dressing with lemon juice, salt, and Worcestershire sauce in a cup; spoon over tuna mixture; toss lightly to mix.
3 Put hamburger buns together with filling, di-

550

viding evenly. Wrap each in foil; place on a cookie sheet.
4 Bake in hot oven (400°) 20 minutes, or until heated through. Remove sandwiches from foil. Serve hot.

Mexicali Cheeseburgers
A top-prize winner in a national contest inspired this grilled three-deck meat-and-cheese sandwich.
Makes 4 servings

    ½ pound ground beef
    ½ cup finely chopped celery
    1 medium-size onion, finely chopped (½ cup)
    1 teaspoon chili powder
    ½ teaspoon sugar
    ½ teaspoon salt
    ⅛ teaspoon pepper
    ⅛ teaspoon garlic powder
    ¼ cup tomato paste (from a 6-ounce can)
    ¼ cup water
    12 slices white sandwich bread
    4 tablespoons (½ stick) soft butter or marga-
      rine
    1 package (8 ounces) sliced process Ameri-
      can cheese

1 Mix ground beef lightly with celery, onion, chili powder, sugar, salt, pepper, and garlic powder until well-blended in a medium-size bowl; shape into a large patty in a medium-size frying pan.

2 Brown 5 minutes on each side, then break up into small chunks; stir in tomato paste and water. Heat to boiling, then simmer 15 minutes to blend flavors.

3 Cut a round from the center of each of 4 of the bread slices with a 3-inch cutter. (Set rounds aside to use for toast or make into croutons for another day.) Spread both sides of remaining 8 slices with butter or margarine.

4 Put each of the 4 sandwiches together this way: Buttered slice of bread, cheese slice, bread slice with center removed, about ⅓ cup meat mixture spooned into center hole, cheese slice, and buttered bread.

5 Sauté in a large heavy frying pan or on a heated griddle, adding more butter or margarine, if needed, 3 to 4 minutes on each side, or until golden and cheese filling melts slightly. Cut each in half diagonally; serve hot.

Ham-and-Egg Clubs

Toasted poppy-seed rolls go together with cheese atop puffs of creamy scrambled eggs, deviled ham, and tomatoes.
Makes 4 servings

4 large poppy-seed rolls
6 tablespoons (¾ stick) butter or margarine
8 eggs
½ cup milk
¼ teaspoon salt
 Dash of pepper
¼ cup chopped green onions
1 can (4½ ounces) deviled ham
2 medium-size tomatoes, sliced
2 slices process American cheese (from an 8-ounce package), each cut into 4 strips

1 Slice each roll crosswise into 3 layers; spread slices with 4 tablespoons of the butter or margarine. (Set remaining aside for scrambling eggs in Step 3.) Place slices in a single layer on rack in broiler pan.

2 Beat eggs with milk, salt, and pepper until foamy in a medium-size bowl; stir in green onions.

3 Melt remaining 2 tablespoons butter or margarine in a medium-size frying pan, tipping pan to coat side; pour in egg mixture. Cook *very slowly*, stirring gently from bottom and side of pan, just until eggs start to set and are creamy-soft; remove from heat.

4 While eggs cook, toast rolls in broiler. Spread middle slices with deviled ham.

5 Layer each sandwich this way: Bottom slice of roll, tomato slices, deviled-ham-spread slice of roll, scrambled eggs. Crisscross 2 cheese strips over each; return to rack of broiler pan.

6 Broil, 4 to 6 inches from heat, 2 to 3 minutes, or just until cheese starts to melt. Serve hot with top slices of rolls, and garnish each with a whole green onion and sweet yellow wax peppers, as pictured, if you wish.

Reubens

They're three decks high with rye bread, corned beef, sauerkraut, tomatoes, and cheese, and are served hot.
Bake at 400° for 20 minutes. Makes 4 servings

¾ cup mayonnaise or salad dressing
¼ cup chili sauce
1 tablespoon chopped parsley
12 slices rye bread
2 medium-size tomatoes, sliced
1 package (8 ounces) sliced caraway cheese, halved
2 packages (4 ounces each) sliced corned beef
1 can (about 1 pound) sauerkraut, well-drained

1 Blend mayonnaise or salad dressing, chili sauce, and parsley in a small bowl. Spread on each slice of rye bread as sandwiches are made.

2 Layer each sandwich this way: Spread bread, tomato and cheese slices, spread bread, corned beef, sauerkraut, and bread, spread side down.

3 Cut each sandwich in half; wrap each two halves in foil; place on a cookie sheet.

4 Bake in hot oven (400°) 20 minutes, or until heated through. Remove sandwiches from foil. Serve hot.

551

Spaghetti Porkers

Heat-and-eat canned spaghetti and sausages with extra seasoning make these whole-meal sandwiches.
Makes 4 servings

1 package (8 ounces) brown 'n' serve sausages, cut in 1-inch pieces
2 cans (15 ounces each) spaghetti in tomato sauce
¾ teaspoon Italian seasoning

4 hero rolls, split and buttered
1 sweet green pepper, seeded and cut in thin rings

1 Brown sausages in a medium-size frying pan; stir in spaghetti and Italian seasoning. Heat slowly, stirring once or twice, until bubbly hot.
2 Put rolls together with spaghetti filling, dividing evenly; top with green-pepper rings; serve with Parmesan cheese to sprinkle over, if you wish.

●

Torpedoes

Golden soufflélike topping takes the place of an extra spread for these meat-and-vegetable-filled rolls.
Makes 4 servings

4 hero rolls
4 tablespoons (½ stick) butter or margarine
1 pound assorted sliced cold cuts
1 sweet red or Bermuda onion, peeled and sliced thin
1 small cucumber, sliced thin
Bottled thin French dressing
1 egg white
¼ cup bottled tartare sauce

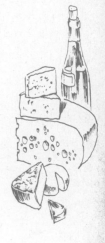

1 Cut each roll in half lengthwise almost to bottom; spread with butter or margarine, then toast.
2 Fold slices of cold cuts and place in rolls; tuck in onion and cucumber slices, dividing evenly. Place rolls on a cookie sheet; drizzle lightly with French dressing.
3 Beat egg white until it stands in firm peaks in a small bowl; fold in tartare sauce. Spoon over filled rolls.
4 Broil, 4 to 6 inches from heat, 5 minutes, or until topping is puffed and lightly golden. Garnish each with chunks of candied dill pickle, pitted ripe olives, and pimiento, threaded onto a wooden pick, as pictured, if you wish. Serve hot.

553

Torpedo, submarine, hero—whatever you call it, this sandwich is quite a line-up. Start out with hero rolls, spread them with butter, lay in an assortment of cold cuts, neatly folded, then tuck in onion and cucumber.

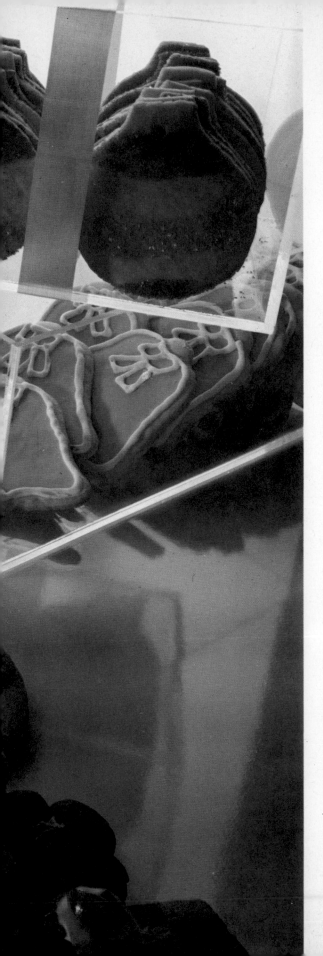

COOKIE JAR

JEWELS

**COOKIE JAR JEWELS:
EASY TRICKS TO SPEED
COOKIE BAKING,
DROP COOKIES, SHAPED
COOKIES, COOKIE PRESS,
COOKIE CUT-OUTS,
REFRIGERATOR COOKIES,
BAR COOKIES**

Cookies are fun to make; cookies are fast; cookies are fabulous; they can be buttery-crisp, wispy as an angel's wing; they can be soft and chewy or chunky and gooey. They can be delicate or spicy, intricate-to-make or easy.

Basically, there are half a dozen different categories of cookies: *drop cookies* (one of the easiest to make because the dough is simply dropped from a spoon onto the baking sheet); *shaped* or *molded* cookies (the dough is worked with the hands, rolled into balls or fingers or little logs or pressed into small molds); *cookie press cookies* (also called *spritz*) for which the dough is forced through a cookie press or pastry tube into a variety of fancy 3-D shapes; *rolled cookies* (these are the enchanting cut-outs, fun to frost and decorate); *refrigerator cookies* (so called because the doughs are shaped into sausage-type links, chilled or frozen, then sliced and baked) and finally, *bar cookies,* really as much cake as cookie because the dough bakes in a loaf pan, then is cut into squares.

The dozens of recipes here, representative of each of the six cookie categories, are among the very best ever developed in the FAMILY CIRCLE kitchens.

555

Just some of the fabulous cookie recipes that follow.

How to be a clever cutup

Ball cookies will be even in size if you pat the dough into a long roll first, then divide it: First in half, then quarters, then eighths, and sixteenths, depending on what size cookie you want.

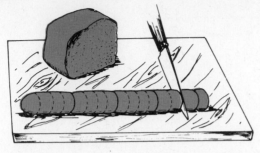

Shape double-good treats this easy way: Make up batches of vanilla and chocolate refrigerator cookie doughs, pat each into a rectangle, stack, chill well, and slice. What could be easier?

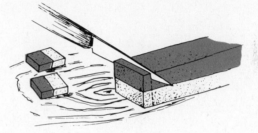

Juice cans make handy molds for refrigerator cookies. Pack dough in the can and chill, then, at baking time, remove the bottom of the can. (Use an opener that cuts a smooth edge.) Press against bottom to push out dough—just enough for one cookie at a time. Cutting against the can helps cookies keep their round shape.

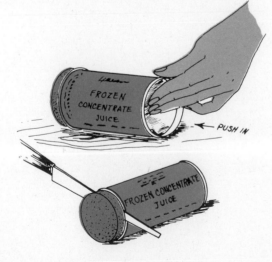

Decorating, assembly-line style

With only one batch of dough, you can make a whole plateful of different-looking, different-tasting treats. Here's how: After shaping the dough, leave some plain, press others, crisscross fashion, with a fork. Make a hollow in some with your thumb or the handle of a wooden spoon to fill with jam or jelly after baking, or top with a big walnut half.

557

Semisweet-chocolate pieces go into and onto cookies.

Store your cookies—right!

Place soft cookies in a canister or box with a tight cover to keep moisture in. Short on containers? Seal cookies in a transparent bag and tuck away in the cupboard. To keep crisp cookies crisp, or fancy cut-outs from breaking, layer with transparent wrap, foil, or wax paper between in a large shallow pan or roaster or on a tray. Bar cookies can stay right in their baking pan tightly covered with foil.

● ● ●

How To Pack Cookies for Mailing

Containers—For sending cookies overseas, use empty metal coffee or shortening cans that come with plastic lids, or metal boxes that are available in variety or housewares stores. Sturdy plastic containers are a satisfactory choice if the cookies are being sent only a short distance. For a bright holiday look, it's fun to cover the container with gaily colored wallpaper or self-adhesive plastic.

Packing—Wrap cookies in pairs, flat sides together, in pieces of foil long enough to allow a generous overlap; seal each with cellophane tape. Cushion the bottom of the container with a layer of crumpled foil and arrange the cookies on top, packing them in as tightly as possible. Stuff any holes between with more foil to keep the cookies from bouncing about. Affix the lid and seal with tape.

Wrapping—Cover the container with a layer of corrugated cardboard, then wrap in a double layer of brown paper. Tie securely with twine or heavy string and affix an address label (typed or printed) on one side only.

558

Four basic types of cookies: a frosted cut-out, a refrigerator pinwheel, a drop cookie crowned with a cherry and a nut-filled spritz wreath.

DROP COOKIES

Chocolate Crisps

You can count on these buttery drops, so rich with brown sugar and bits of chocolate, to disappear fast.
Bake at 350° for 10 minutes. Makes about 5 dozen

2¼ cups sifted all-purpose flour
1 teaspoon baking soda
1 teaspoon salt
½ cup (1 stick) butter or margarine
½ cup vegetable shortening
1 cup firmly packed brown sugar
½ cup granulated sugar
2 eggs
1 tablespoon rum flavoring or extract
1 package (12 ounces) semisweet-chocolate pieces

1 Measure flour, soda, and salt into a sifter.
2 Cream butter or margarine and shortening with brown and granulated sugars until fluffy in a large bowl; beat in eggs and rum flavoring or extract.
3 Sift in flour mixture, a third at a time, blending well to make a soft dough. Stir in semisweet-chocolate pieces. Drop by rounded teaspoonfuls, about 2 inches apart, on ungreased cookie sheets.
4 Bake in moderate oven (350°) 10 minutes, or until lightly golden. Remove from cookie sheets; cool completely on wire racks.

Butterscotch Crispies

Dainty wisps of goodness.
Bake at 325° for 5 to 8 minutes. Makes about 10 dozen tiny cookies

1 egg
¼ cup granulated sugar
¼ cup brown sugar, firmly packed
2 tablespoons all-purpose flour
Dash of salt
½ teaspoon vanilla
½ cup finely chopped walnuts
¼ cup finely chopped mixed candied fruits

1 Beat egg until light in small bowl; beat in sugars; stir in flour, salt, vanilla, walnuts, and fruits.
2 Drop batter in tiny mounds from tip of knife about 1½ inches apart on well-greased cookie sheets. (Mounds should be about the size of small grapes.)

3 Bake in slow oven (325°) 5 to 8 minutes, or until golden.
4 Remove from cookie sheets with spatula; cool on wire cake racks.

Ginger Jumbos

They'll remind you of big puffs of gingerbread—soft, light, and spicy. What a treat with milk, tea, or hot chocolate.
Bake at 400° for 8 minutes. Makes about 2 dozen

2¼ cups sifted all-purpose flour
2 teaspoons baking soda
1 teaspoon ground cinnamon
½ teaspoon ground ginger
¼ teaspoon salt
½ cup (1 stick) butter or margarine
⅓ cup sugar
⅔ cup molasses
1 egg
½ cup milk
1½ teaspoons vinegar
Walnut halves

1 Measure flour, soda, cinnamon, ginger, and salt into sifter.
2 Cream butter or margarine with sugar until fluffy in large bowl; beat in molasses and egg. Combine milk and vinegar in 1-cup measure.
3 Sift dry ingredients, adding alternately with milk mixture, a third at a time, into molasses mixture, blending well after each to make a thick batter.
4 Drop by rounded tablespoonfuls, 2 inches apart, on greased cookie sheets; top each with a walnut half.
5 Bake in hot oven (400°) 8 minutes, or until centers spring back when lightly pressed with fingertip. Remove from cookie sheets; cool completely on wire racks.

559

Sour-Cream Softies

Cinnamon-sugar "frosts" the tops of these big, old-fashioned puffs.
Bake at 400° for 12 minutes. Makes about 3½ dozen

3 cups sifted all-purpose flour
1 teaspoon salt
½ teaspoon baking powder
½ teaspoon baking soda
½ cup (1 stick) butter or margarine

1½ cups sugar
2 eggs
1 teaspoon vanilla
1 cup (8-ounce carton) dairy sour cream
  Cinnamon-sugar

1 Measure flour, salt, baking powder, and soda into a sifter.
2 Cream butter or margarine with sugar until well-blended in a large bowl; beat in eggs and vanilla. Sift in flour mixture, adding alternately with sour cream and blending well to make a thick batter.
3 Drop by rounded tablespoonfuls, 4 inches apart, on greased cookie sheets; spread into 2-inch rounds; sprinkle with cinnamon-sugar.
4 Bake in hot oven (400°) 12 minutes, or until lightly golden around edges. Remove from cookie sheets; cool completely on wire racks.

Oatmeal Crunchies

They're crisp and chewy with a good rich butterscotch flavor.
Bake at 375° for 12 minutes. Makes about 3½ dozen

1½ cups sifted all-purpose flour
½ teaspoon baking soda
½ teaspoon salt
  Dash of ground mace
1 cup vegetable shortening
1¼ cups firmly packed brown sugar
1 egg
¼ cup milk
1¾ cups quick-cooking rolled oats
1 cup chopped walnuts

1 Measure flour, soda, salt, and mace into a sifter.
2 Cream shortening with brown sugar until fluffy in a large bowl; beat in egg and milk. Sift in flour mixture, blending well to make a thick batter; fold in rolled oats and walnuts.

3 Drop by teaspoonfuls, 3 inches apart, on greased cookie sheets.
4 Bake in moderate oven (375°) 12 minutes, or until lightly golden. Remove from cookie sheets; cool completely on wire racks.

Butterscotch-Oatmeal Crunchies

Bite into these spicy rich cookies and you'll find tiny pieces of butterscotch-flavor "candy."
Bake at 400° for 14 minutes. Makes about 5 dozen

2½ cups sifted all-purpose flour
1 teaspoon baking soda
1 teaspoon salt
1 teaspoon pumpkin-pie spice
½ teaspoon baking powder
¾ cup vegetable shortening
1½ cups sugar
2 eggs
1 teaspoon vanilla
½ cup water
2 cups quick-cooking rolled oats
1 package (about 6 ounces) butterscotch-flavor pieces

1 Measure flour, soda, salt, pumpkin-pie spice, and baking powder into a sifter.
2 Cream shortening with sugar until fluffy in a large bowl; beat in eggs and vanilla.
3 Sift in flour mixture, a third at a time, adding alternately with water, and blending well to make a soft dough. Stir in rolled oats and but-

560

Chunky, chewy drop cookies are what children adore.

terscotch-flavor pieces. Drop by rounded teaspoonfuls, about 2 inches apart, on ungreased
cookie sheets.
4 Bake in hot oven (400°) 14 minutes, or until
lightly golden. Remove from cookie sheets; cool
completely on wire racks.

Cereal Crisps
Bake at 350° for 12 minutes. Makes about 4½
dozen

1½ cups sifted all-purpose flour
½ teaspoon baking soda
½ teaspoon salt
1¾ cup (1½ sticks) butter or margarine
1 cup granulated sugar
½ cup firmly packed brown sugar
1 egg
1 teaspoon vanilla
1 cup oven-toasted rice cereal
½ cup quick-cooking rolled oats
1 cup chopped pecans

1 Sift flour, soda, and salt onto wax paper.
2 Cream butter or margarine with granulated
and brown sugars until fluffy in a large bowl;
beat in egg and vanilla.
3 Stir in flour mixture until well-blended, then
rice cereal, rolled oats, and pecans.
4 Drop by teaspoonfuls, 2 inches apart, on
ungreased cookie sheets.
5 Bake in moderate oven (350°) 12 minutes,
or until lightly golden. Remove from cookie
sheets to wire racks; cool.

Mint Drops
Bake at 375° for 10 minutes. Makes about 4
dozen

2 cups sifted all-purpose flour
¾ teaspoon baking soda
½ teaspoon salt
1 cup (2 sticks) butter or margarine
½ cup granulated sugar
½ cup firmly packed brown sugar
2 eggs
1 package (6 ounces) semisweet-choco-
   late-mint pieces
1 cup chopped walnuts

1 Sift flour, soda, and salt onto wax paper.

2 Cream butter or margarine with granulated
and brown sugars until fluffy in a medium-size
bowl; beat in eggs.
3 Stir in flour mixture, a third at a time, until
well-blended; fold in chocolate pieces and walnuts.
4 Drop by teaspoonfuls, 2 inches apart, on
ungreased cookie sheets.
5 Bake in moderate oven (375°) 10 minutes,
or until lightly golden. Remove from cookie
sheets to wire racks; cool.

Brown-Edge Spicies
Bake at 350° about 12 minutes. Makes about
3 dozen

2 cups sifted all-purpose flour
1 teaspoon baking powder
½ teaspoon baking soda
½ teaspoon salt
½ teaspoon ground cinnamon
½ teaspoon ground nutmeg
¼ teaspoon ground cloves
½ cup vegetable shortening
1 cup sugar
1 egg
1 teaspoon vanilla
1 cup canned applesauce

1 Measure flour, baking powder, baking soda,
salt, cinnamon, nutmeg, and ground cloves into
sifter; save for Step 4.
2 Cream shortening until soft in medium-size
bowl; add sugar gradually, creaming after each
addition until well-blended.
3 Stir in egg and vanilla; beat until mixture is
light and fluffy.
4 Sift and add dry ingredients alternately with
applesauce, blending well after each addition.
5 Drop batter by heaping teaspoonfuls onto
lightly greased cookie sheets, keeping mounds
2 inches apart.
6 Bake in moderate oven (350°) about 12 minutes, or until cookies are lightly browned around
edges.
7 Loosen at once from cookie sheet by running
spatula under each cookie; cool on wire cake
racks.
8 Store cookies in cookie jar or airtight container to keep them soft.

Brown-Edge Lemon Wafers
Bake at 375° about 10 minutes. Makes about
5 dozen

¼ cup sugar (for topping)

561

Grated rind of ½ lemon (for topping)
2 cups sifted all-purpose flour
2 teaspoons baking powder
½ teaspoon salt
½ cup vegetable shortening
1 cup sugar (for dough)
1 egg
Grated rind of 1 lemon (for dough)
½ teaspoon vanilla
½ cup water
¼ cup lemon juice

1 Blend sugar and lemon rind (for topping) in cup; save for Step 6.
2 Measure flour, baking powder, and salt into sifter.
3 Cream shortening until soft in medium-size bowl; add sugar (for dough) gradually, creaming well.
4 Blend in egg, lemon rind (for dough), and vanilla; beat until mixture is light and fluffy.
5 Sift dry ingredients; add alternately with water and lemon juice, blending until smooth after each addition. (Dough will be very soft.)
6 Drop dough by teaspoonfuls 2 inches apart on greased cookie sheets; sprinkle tops lightly with lemon-sugar mixture.
7 Bake in moderate oven (375°) about 10 minutes, or until edges of cookies are light brown.
8 Run spatula under cookies to loosen from sheet; cool on wire racks.

Penny Wafers
A recipe your friends will ask for.
Bake at 425° for 5 minutes. Makes about 10 dozen tiny cookies

2 tablespoons currants
1 tablespoon hot water
2 teaspoons rum flavoring
4 tablespoons (½ stick) butter or margarine
¼ cup sugar
1 egg
⅓ cup sifted all-purpose flour

1 Combine currants, hot water, and rum flavoring in small bowl; let stand about 1 hour to blend flavors.
2 Cream butter or margarine until soft in medium-size bowl; blend in sugar, then egg, beating until light and fluffy; stir in flour and currant mixture.
3 Drop batter in tiny mounds from tip of knife

about 1½ inches apart on well-greased cookie sheet. (Mounds should be about the size of small grapes.)
4 Bake in hot oven (425°) 5 minutes, or until edges are golden.
5 Remove from cookie sheet with spatula; cool on wire cake racks.

Taffy Rolls
Shattery bits of butter-nut goodness. They break easily, so pack carefully.
Bake at 300° for 10 minutes. Makes about 6 dozen

½ cup (1 stick) butter or margarine
1 cup firmly packed brown sugar
2 eggs
½ cup finely chopped pecans
¼ cup sifted all-purpose flour
½ teaspoon salt

1 Cream butter or margarine until soft in medium-size bowl; gradually add sugar, creaming well after each addition until light and fluffy.
2 Beat in eggs, one at a time, beating well after each addition; stir in nuts, flour, and salt.
3 Drop batter by small teaspoonfuls about 5 inches apart on lightly greased cookie sheet; spread thinly. Work with only 6 cookies at a time for easier handling.
4 Bake in slow oven (300°) 10 minutes, or until golden-brown.
5 Cool cookies on cookie sheet 3 minutes, or just until firm enough to hold their shape. (When hot from the oven they are too soft to handle.)
6 Loosen, one at a time, with spatula; quickly roll around handle of wooden spoon; place on wire cake rack to cool and crisp. While shaping, if cookies become too brittle, slide pan into oven for 30 seconds to soften them.
7 Bake and shape remaining cookies until all dough is used.

Parisiennes
They're rich-as-rich meringue cookies, each crowned with a chocolate topknot.
Bake at 275° for 20 minutes. Makes about 10 dozen

3 egg whites
1 tablespoon cider vinegar
½ teaspoon salt
1 cup sugar
4 squares, semisweet chocolate, grated

1 cup finely chopped almonds
1 cup (6-ounce package) semisweet-chocolate
  pieces
1 tablespoon vegetable shortening
¼ cup finely chopped pistachio nuts

1 Beat egg whites with vinegar and salt until foamy in large bowl. Beat in sugar, 1 tablespoon at a time, until meringue stands in firm peaks. (This will take about 10 minutes.) *Gently* fold in grated chocolate, and almonds.
2 Drop by half-teaspoonfuls, 1 inch apart, on lightly greased cookie sheets.
3 Bake in very slow oven (275°) 20 minutes, or just until set. Remove carefully from cookie sheets; cool.
4 Melt semisweet-chocolate pieces with shortening in top of double boiler over hot water. Swirl on tops of cookies; sprinkle with nuts.

Currant Saucies
Applesauce, spice, and everything nice goes into these tiny thin drop cookies.
Bake at 350° for 10 minutes. Makes 10 dozen

1 cup sifted all-purpose flour
½ teaspoon baking powder
½ teaspoon pumpkin-pie spice
¼ teaspoon baking soda
¼ teaspoon salt
⅓ cup butter or margarine
½ cup sugar
1 egg
½ teaspoon vanilla
½ cup canned applesauce
3 tablespoons milk
¼ cup currants

1 Measure dry ingredients into sifter.
2 Cream butter or margarine with sugar until light in medium-size bowl; beat in egg and vanilla; stir in applesauce. Sift in dry ingredients, alternately with milk; stir in currants. (Batter will be thin.)
3 Drop by half-teaspoonfuls, about 2 inches apart, on greased cookie sheets.
4 Bake in moderate oven (350°) 10 minutes, or until lightly browned around edges. Remove from cookie sheets; cool completely on wire racks.

Tile Cookies
Bake at 375° for 5 minutes. Makes about 12 dozen

1⅓ cups sifted all-purpose flour
1 teaspoon baking powder
¼ teaspoon salt
4 tablespoons (½ stick) butter or margarine
¾ cup granulated sugar
2 eggs
1 teaspoon vanilla
2 tablespoons milk
  Red decorating sugar

1 Sift flour, baking powder, and salt onto wax paper.
2 Cream butter or margarine with granulated sugar until fluffy-light in a medium-size bowl; beat in 1 of the eggs and vanilla. Stir in flour mixture, a third at a time, alternately with milk, blending well to make a soft dough.
3 Drop dough, ½ teaspoonful at a time, 2 inches apart, onto greased large cookie sheets; spread into 1½-inch rounds. Beat remaining egg well in a small bowl; brush lightly over each round; sprinkle with red sugar. (For easy handling, bake only 6 cookies at a time, for they must be shaped while hot.)
4 Bake in moderate oven (375°) 5 minutes, or just until lightly browned around edges. Carefully remove at once from cookie sheets and press each around the handle of a wooden spoon. Place on wire racks; cool completely. (If cookies become too brittle to shape easily, return cookie sheet to oven for 30 seconds to soften them.)

Fruit Cake Drops
Bake at 350° for 12 minutes. Makes about 12 dozen

1 cup sifted all-purpose flour
¼ teaspoon baking soda
¼ teaspoon salt
½ teaspoon ground cinnamon
4 tablespoons (½ stick) butter or margarine
½ cup sugar
1 egg
2 tablespoons brandy
1 package (8 ounces) pitted dates, chopped
1 container (4 ounces) mixed candied fruits,
  chopped
1 container (4 ounces) candied red cherries,
  chopped
1 container (4 ounces) candied pineapple,
  chopped
½ cup chopped blanched almonds
½ cup chopped Brazil nuts

563

1 Sift flour, soda, salt, and cinnamon onto wax paper.
2 Cream butter or margarine with sugar until fluffy-light in a medium-size bowl; beat in egg and brandy.
3 Stir in flour mixture, half at a time, blending well to make a soft dough. Stir in dates, candied fruits, almonds, and Brazil nuts.
4 Drop batter, a rounded teaspoonful at a time, 1 inch apart, onto lightly greased cookie sheets.
5 Bake in moderate oven (350°) 12 minutes, or until firm and lightly browned. Remove from cookie sheets to wire racks; cool completely.

Toasty Macaroons

Bake at 325° for 15 minutes. Makes about 3 dozen

> 2 cans (4½ ounces each) toasted sweetened coconut
> ⅔ cup sweetened condensed milk (from a 14-ounce can)
> 1 teaspoon rum extract
> ¼ teaspoon ground ginger
> Red and green candied cherries, sliced

1 Combine coconut, sweetened condensed milk, rum extract, and ginger in a medium-size bowl. Stir mixture until well-blended.
2 Drop by teaspoonfuls onto foil-lined large cookie sheet. Garnish each cookie with a slice of candied cherry.
3 Bake in slow oven (325°) 15 minutes, or until macaroons are firm. Remove from cookie sheet to wire racks. Cool completely.

Button Macaroons

564

Crisp and chewy, these sweets keep well, so you can make them ahead of the rush.
Bake at 325° for 15 minutes. Makes about 5 dozen tiny cookies

> 1 egg, separated
> ⅓ cup sugar
> 1 teaspoon baking powder
> ⅛ teaspoon salt
> ¼ teaspoon vanilla
> ¾ cup quick-cooking rolled oats
> ½ cup coconut (from an about-4-ounce can)
> 1 tablespoon butter or margarine, melted
> Candied red and green cherries, cut in slivers

1 Beat egg white until foamy-white and double in volume in a small bowl; beat in 3 tablespoons of the sugar, 1 tablespoon at a time, until meringue stands in firm peaks.
2 Beat egg yolk well in a medium-size bowl; beat in remaining sugar until fluffy-light. Stir in baking powder, salt, vanilla, rolled oats, coconut, and melted butter or margarine; fold in meringue.
3 Drop by half teaspoonfuls, 1 inch apart, onto greased cookie sheets; decorate each with slivered red and green cherries.
4 Bake in slow oven (325°) 15 minutes, or until firm and lightly golden. Remove from cookie sheets; cool completely on wire racks. Store in a tightly covered container.

Meringue Miniatures

Airy little wisps all aglitter with colored-sugar toppings.
Bake at 250° for 45 minutes. Makes 5 dozen

> 2 egg whites
> 1 teaspoon white vinegar
> Dash of salt
> ½ teaspoon almond extract
> ½ teaspoon vanilla
> ½ cup sugar
> Red food coloring
> Colored decorating sugars

1 Beat egg whites with vinegar and salt until foamy-white and double in volume in medium-size bowl; beat in almond extract and vanilla.
2 Sprinkle in sugar *very slowly*, 1 tablespoon at a time, beating all the time until sugar is completely dissolved and meringue stands in firm peaks. Beating will take about 25 minutes in all with an electric beater. (You can test if sugar is dissolved by rubbing a bit of meringue between fingers. It should feel perfectly smooth—not grainy.)
3 Spoon half of mixture into a second medium-size bowl; blend in a few drops red food coloring to tint a delicate pink; leave remaining plain.
4 Drop by teaspoonfuls, 1 inch apart, on brown-paper-lined cookie sheets; sprinkle with colored decorating sugars.
5 Bake in very slow oven (250°) 45 minutes, or until crisp. Remove cookies on brown paper to wire rack; cool completely; remove from paper. Keep tightly covered, for they absorb moisture.

More cookie types: shaped cookies (left), bars (center), cut-outs (top), drop cookies (top, bottom right).

Chocolate Meringues
Bake at 275° for 25 minutes. Makes 6 dozen

3 egg whites
½ teaspoon salt
⅛ teaspoon cream of tartar
1 cup sugar
1 cup very finely chopped blanched almonds
4 squares (4 ounces) unsweetened chocolate, grated
1 can milk chocolate creamy-type frosting
    Green candied cherries, slivered

1 Beat egg whites with salt and cream of tartar until foamy-white and double in volume in a large bowl. Sprinkle in sugar, 1 tablespoon at a time, beating all the time, until sugar completely dissolves and meringue stands in firm peaks. Gently fold in almonds and chocolate.
2 Drop by teaspoonfuls, one inch apart, on lightly greased large cookie sheets (or press through pastry bag fitted with a large plain tip).
3 Bake in very slow oven (275°) 25 minutes, or until firmly set. Remove carefully from cookie sheets to wire racks; cool completely.
4 Decorate each meringue with a swirl of frosting and a sliver of green cherry.

Florentine Rollups
Lacelike, shattery-crisp, and almost as rich as taffy candy, with now-and-then bites of fruit and almonds.
Bake at 300° for 10 to 12 minutes. Makes about 3 dozen

¾ cup sugar
½ cup cream for whipping
4 tablespoons (½ stick) butter or margarine
1 egg white, slightly beaten
¾ cup finely chopped almonds
2 tablespoons finely chopped red candied cherries
2 tablespoons finely chopped green candied cherries
2 tablespoons finely chopped citron
¼ cup sifted all-purpose flour

1 Combine sugar, cream, butter or margarine, beaten egg white, almonds, cherries, and citron in a medium-size saucepan. Heat slowly, stirring constantly, just until butter or margarine melts and mixture bubbles up. Cool to room temperature, then stir in flour. (Mixture will be medium-thick.)
2 Drop by rounded teaspoonfuls, 5 inches

565

Who wouldn't welcome Lacy Molasses Rollups, Shortbread, cherry or chocolate trimmed macaroons?

apart, on greased cookie sheets; spread into very thin 4-inch rounds. (Work with not more than 3 cookies at a time, for they must be rolled while hot.)

3 Bake in slow oven (300°) 10 to 12 minutes, or until a rich brown.

4 Cool on cookie sheet 1 minute, or just until firm enough to hold their shape. (Right from the oven, they are too soft to handle.)

5 Loosen, 1 at a time, with a spatula, but do not remove from cookie sheet. Quickly roll each around the handle of a wooden spoon or pencil to make a cylinder; place on a wire rack; let cool 1 to 2 minutes, or until firm. Carefully slip off spoon handle or pencil and cool cookies completely. (If cookies become too brittle to shape, slide cookie sheet back into the oven for 30 seconds, and cookies will soften.)

Nearly everyone's favorite: classic Toll House Cookies.

Lacy Molasses Rollups
They're almost like candy, and though they take a little time, they're so worth it!
Bake at 325° for 10 minutes. Makes about 4 dozen

¾ *cup sugar*
½ *cup molasses*
⅓ *cup water*
¾ *cup (1½ sticks) butter or margarine*
1¼ *cups sifted all-purpose flour*
1½ *teaspoons baking powder*
½ *teaspoon salt*
¼ *teaspoon cinnamon*
1 *cup finely chopped walnuts*

1 Combine sugar, molasses, water, and butter or margarine in large saucepan. Heat slowly, stirring constantly, just to boiling; cool slightly.

2 Sift flour, baking powder, salt, and cinnamon into small bowl; stir in walnuts to coat well. (Be sure walnuts have been chopped finely or cookies will crack when rolled.) Stir into molasses mixture just until blended. (Mixture will be very thin.)

3 Drop by scant tablespoonfuls, 3 inches apart, on greased cookie sheets. (Make only 6 cookies at a time for easy handling. To save time, use two cookie sheets and bake one batch while shaping the other.)

4 Bake in slow oven (325°) 10 minutes, or until a rich dark brown. Cool on cookie sheet 1 minute, or just until firm enough to handle.

5 Loosen with spatula but do not remove from cookie sheet. Quickly roll into a cylinder with fingers; place, seam side down, on wire racks to cool and crisp. (If cookies become too brittle to shape easily, return cookie sheet to oven for 30 seconds to soften them.) These dainties do not store well. Enjoy them!

Toll House Cookies
Bake at 375° for 10 to 12 minutes. Makes about 4 dozen cookies

1 *cup plus 2 tablespoons sifted all-purpose flour*
½ *teaspoon baking soda*
¼ *teaspoon salt*
½ *cup butter or margarine*
⅓ *cup plus 1 tablespoon granulated sugar*
⅓ *cup plus 1 tablespoon firmly packed light brown sugar*
1 *teaspoon vanilla*
1 *egg*
1 *package (6 ounces) semisweet-chocolate pieces*
⅔ *cup chopped pecans*

1 Sift flour, baking soda and salt onto a piece of wax paper.

2 Cream butter or margarine, sugars and vanilla until light and fluffy. Beat in egg.

3 Mix in dry ingredients; stir in chocolate pieces and pecans.

4 Drop onto lightly greased cookie sheets, spacing cookies about 2 inches apart. Bake 10 to 12 minutes until lightly browned around the edges. Transfer to wire racks to cool. Store in an airtight cannister.

567

Daisies

Bake at 350° for 10 minutes. Makes about 9 dozen cookies

1 cup sifted all-purpose flour
½ teaspoon baking powder
  Dash of salt
4 tablespoons (½ stick) butter or margarine
½ cup sugar
1 egg
½ teaspoon vanilla
2 tablespoons milk
  Plain chocolate-candy wafers

1 Sift flour, baking powder, and salt onto wax paper.
2 Cream butter or margarine with sugar until fluffy-light in a medium-size bowl; beat in egg and vanilla. Stir in flour mixture, half at a time, alternately with milk, blending well to make a very soft dough.
3 Drop dough, a level half-teaspoonful at a time, 2 inches apart, onto lightly greased cookie sheets; press a candy wafer into center of each mound.
4 Bake in moderate oven (350°) 10 minutes, or just until golden around edges. Remove at once from cookie sheets to wire racks; cool completely.

Chocolate-Pecan Rounds

Wheat germ adds a nutlike extra flavor to these crisp sweet treats.
Bake at 350° for 10 minutes. Makes about 5 dozen

1½ cups sifted all-purpose flour
½ teaspoon baking soda
¼ teaspoon salt
½ cup regular wheat germ
1 cup coarsely chopped pecans
2 squares unsweetened chocolate
½ cup (1 stick) butter or margarine
½ cup granulated sugar
½ cup firmly packed light brown sugar
1 egg
⅓ cup milk
2 teaspoons vanilla

1 Sift flour, soda, and salt into a medium-size bowl; stir in wheat germ and pecans.
2 Melt chocolate with butter or margarine in the top of a double boiler over simmering water; pour into a large bowl. Cool to lukewarm.

3 Beat granulated and brown sugars into chocolate mixture; beat in egg, milk, and vanilla. Stir in flour mixture until well-blended. Drop by rounded teaspoonsful onto lightly greased cookie sheets.
4 Bake in moderate oven (350°) 10 minutes, or until firm. Remove from cookie sheets to wire racks; cool completely.

Banana-Date Puffs

Soft, moist, and spicy. They'll remind you somewhat of little cakes.
Bake at 375° for 10 minutes. Makes about 5 dozen

3 cups sifted all-purpose flour
1 teaspoon baking soda
1 teaspoon pumpkin-pie spice
½ teaspoon salt
¾ cup (1½ sticks) butter or margarine
¾ cup firmly packed light brown sugar
1 egg
2 medium-size ripe bananas, mashed (1 cup)
1 teaspoon vanilla
1 cup chopped dates

1 Sift flour, soda, pumpkin-pie spice, and salt onto wax paper.
2 Cream butter or margarine with brown sugar until fluffy-light in a large bowl; beat in egg, mashed bananas, and vanilla. Stir in flour mixture, half at a time, until well-blended; stir in dates. Drop by rounded teaspoonsful onto lightly greased cookie sheets.
3 Bake in moderate oven (375°) 10 minutes, or until firm and lightly golden around edges. Remove from cookie sheets to wire racks; cool completely.

Cherry-Coconut Chews

For lunch boxes, teatime, or dessert with fruit or sherbet, they're winners!
Bake at 375° for 10 minutes. Makes about 4½ dozen

2 cups sifted all-purpose flour
½ teaspoon baking powder
½ teaspoon baking soda
½ teaspoon salt
⅔ cup vegetable shortening
⅔ cup sugar
1 egg
½ cup milk

1 teaspoon vanilla
1 cup flaked coconut
¼ cup chopped maraschino cherries, drained

1 Sift flour, baking powder, soda, and salt onto wax paper.
2 Cream shortening with sugar until fluffy-light in a large bowl; beat in egg, milk, and vanilla. Stir in flour mixture until well-blended; stir in coconut and cherries. Drop by rounded teaspoonsful onto lightly greased cookie sheets.
3 Bake in moderate oven (375°) 10 minutes, or until firm and lightly golden around edges. Remove from cookie sheets to wire racks; cool completely.

Sesame Lace Wafers
More candy than cookie, these crispies are fragile and call for careful handling.
Bake at 325° for 10 minutes. Makes about 12 dozen

½ cup sifted all-purpose flour
½ teaspoon baking powder
  Dash of salt
¼ cup granulated sugar
¼ cup dark corn syrup
4 tablespoons (½ stick) butter or margarine
1 tablespoon water
¼ cup sesame seeds
  Colored decorating sugar

1 Measure flour, baking powder, and salt into a sifter.
2 Combine granulated sugar, corn syrup, butter or margarine, and water in a small saucepan. Heat, stirring constantly, to boiling, then cook, stirring often, 5 minutes; remove from heat. Cool 5 minutes.
3 Sift flour mixture over syrup in pan, then stir in; stir in sesame seeds.
4 Drop by ¼ teaspoonfuls, 3 inches apart, onto greased cookie sheets. (Dough will spread, bubble, and become lacelike as it bakes.)
5 Bake in slow oven (325°) 10 minutes, or until brown. Sprinkle with colored sugar. Let stand on cookie sheets on wire racks 1 minute to firm, then remove carefully to racks; cool completely.

SHAPED COOKIES

Chocolate Walnut Wafers
These fudgy rounds sparkle prettily with a sugary coating—and shaping's so easy.
Bake at 350° for 12 minutes. Makes 4 dozen

2 cups sifted all-purpose flour
1 teaspoon baking powder
½ teaspoon salt
¼ teaspoon baking soda
¾ cup (1½ sticks) butter or margarine
¾ cup firmly packed brown sugar
2 squares unsweetened chocolate, melted
1 egg
1 teaspoon vanilla
¼ cup milk
  Granulated sugar
  Walnut halves

1 Measure flour, baking powder, salt, and baking soda into sifter.
2 Cream butter or margarine and brown sugar until fluffy in medium-size bowl; beat in melted chocolate, egg, vanilla, and milk. Sift in dry ingredients, a third at a time, blending well to make a soft dough. Chill several hours, or until firm enough to handle.
3 Roll dough, a heaping teaspoonful at a time, into marble-size balls between palms of hands; roll in granulated sugar in pie plate. Place, 3 inches apart, on ungreased cookie sheets; flatten to ¼-inch thickness with bottom of glass. Top each with a walnut half.
4 Bake in moderate oven (350°) 12 minutes, or until firm. Remove carefully from cookie sheets; cool on wire racks. Store in container with tight-fitting cover.

Snowballs
Buttery snow-white puffs that literally melt in your mouth—and one just teases you into having another.
Bake at 325° for 20 minutes. Makes 4 dozen

½ cup (1 stick) butter or margarine
3 tablespoons 10X (confectioners' powdered) sugar
1 cup sifted all-purpose flour
1 cup finely chopped pecans
  10X (confectioners' powdered) sugar

1 Cream butter or margarine and 3 tablespoons 10X sugar until fluffy in medium-size bowl; stir in flour gradually, then pecans until well-blended. Chill several hours, or until firm enough to handle.
2 Roll dough, a teaspoonful at a time, into mar-

569

ble-size balls between palms of hands; place, 2 inches apart, on ungreased cookie sheets.

3 Bake in slow oven (325°) 20 minutes, or until lightly golden.

4 Cool on cookie sheets 5 minutes; remove carefully. Roll in 10X sugar in pie plate while still warm to make a generous white coating; cool completely on wire racks. Store with wax paper or transparent wrap between layers in container with tight-fitting cover.

Chocolate Snowballs

They're sugary-white outside, dark chocolate inside. Bake some to pack for gifts.
Bake at 350° for 8 minutes. Makes about 5 dozen

2 cups sifted all-purpose flour
1 teaspoon baking powder
½ teaspoon salt
¼ teaspoon baking soda
¾ cup (1½ sticks) butter or margarine
¾ cup firmly packed brown sugar
2 squares unsweetened chocolate, melted
1 egg
1 teaspoon vanilla
¼ cup milk
  10X (confectioners' powdered) sugar

1 Measure dry ingredients into sifter.

2 Cream butter or margarine with brown sugar until light in medium-size bowl; beat in melted chocolate, egg, vanilla, and milk. Sift in dry ingredients, a little at a time, blending well to make a stiff dough. Chill overnight, or until firm enough to handle.

3 Roll dough, a teaspoonful at a time, into marble-size balls; place about 2 inches apart on ungreased cookie sheets.

4 Bake in moderate oven (350°) 8 minutes, or until tops are crackled. Remove carefully from cookie sheets; roll in 10X sugar while still hot. Cool on wire racks, then roll again in 10X sugar to make a generous white coating.

570

Butternut Crescents

A cookie lover's dream come true, for these are nut-packed, melt-away morsels.
Bake at 300° for 20 minutes. Makes about 6 dozen

1 cup (2 sticks) butter or margarine
¼ cup 10X (confectioners' powdered) sugar
  (for dough)

1 tablespoon water
2 teaspoons vanilla
2 cups sifted all-purpose flour
1 cup finely chopped pecans
  10X (confectioners' powdered) sugar (for coating)

1 Melt butter or margarine in small suacepan; remove from heat. Stir in ¼ cup 10X sugar, water, and vanilla; gradually blend in flour, then pecans, to make a pastrylike dough.

2 Pinch off dough, about a teaspoonful at a time, and roll lightly between palms of hands into fingerlike strips about 2 inches long. Place on ungreased cookie sheets; curve into crescents.

3 Bake in slow oven (300°) 20 minutes, or until delicately golden.

4 Remove carefully from cookie sheets; dust with 10X sugar while still hot. Cool on wire rack, then dust again with 10X sugar to make a generous white coating.

Butternut Moons

Shape half of the dough for BUTTERNUT CRESCENTS into small balls, like fat full moons, then bake the same as CRESCENTS. Decorate cooled balls with a dollop of PECAN COCOA CREAM (recipe follows); press a pecan half into soft frosting.

  PECAN-COCOA CREAM—Blend ¼ cup unsifted 10X (confectioners' powdered) sugar, 2 teaspoons dry cocoa, 2 teaspoons milk, and 1 teaspoon melted butter or margarine until creamy-smooth in 1-cup measure. Makes enough for 3 dozen.

Cookie-Jar Gingersnaps

Bake at 350° for 12 to 15 minutes. Makes about 4 dozen

2 cups sifted all-purpose flour
1 tablespoon ground ginger
2 teaspoons baking soda
1 teaspoon ground cinnamon
½ teaspoon salt
¾ cup vegetable shortening
1 cup sugar
1 egg, unbeaten
¼ cup molasses
  Granulated sugar

1 Measure flour, ginger, baking soda, cinnamon, and salt into sifter; sift 2 times onto wax paper; return to sifter.

Yule favorites—Chocolate Walnut Wafers, Snowballs. ▶

2 Cream shortening until soft in medium-size bowl; add sugar gradually, creaming after each addition until mixture is well-blended.
3 Beat in egg and molasses.
4 Sift dry ingredients over creamed mixture; blend well.
5 Form teaspoonfuls of dough into small balls by rolling them lightly, one at a time, between palms of hands. Roll dough balls in granulated sugar to cover entire outside surface; place 2 inches apart on ungreased cookie sheets.
6 Bake in moderate oven (350°) 12 to 15 minutes, or until tops are slightly rounded, crackly, and lightly browned.
7 Run spatula under cookies to loosen from sheets; cool on wire racks.

Chocolate Crinkle Puffs

A shower of sugar makes these fudgy charmers crackle prettily on top as they bake. Tuck a few into lunch boxes for a surprise.
Bake at 350° for 8 minutes. Makes about 5 dozen

    2 cups sifted all-purpose flour
    1 teaspoon baking powder
    ½ teaspoon salt
    ¼ teaspoon baking soda
    ¾ cup (1½ sticks) butter or margarine
    ¾ cup firmly packed brown sugar
    2 squares unsweetened chocolate, melted
    1 egg
    1 teaspoon vanilla
    ¼ cup milk
      Granulated sugar

1 Measure flour, baking powder, salt, and soda into sifter.
2 Cream butter or margarine with brown sugar until fluffy in medium-size bowl; beat in melted chocolate, egg, vanilla, and milk.
3 Sift in dry ingredients, a third at a time, blending well to make a stiff dough.
4 Roll dough, a teaspoonful at a time, into marble-size balls; roll in granulated sugar; place about 2 inches apart on ungreased cookie sheets.
5 Bake in moderate oven (350°) 8 minutes, or until tops are crackled. Remove carefully from cookie sheets; cool on wire racks.

Shortbread Cookies

Bake at 300° for 25 minutes. Makes about 5 dozen

572

    1 cup (2 sticks) butter or margarine
    ½ cup sugar
    ½ teaspoon lemon extract
    2½ cups sifted all-purpose flour
      DECORATOR'S ICING (recipe follows)

1 Beat butter or margarine with sugar until fluffy-light in a large bowl. Beat in lemon extract. Stir in flour, a third at a time, blending well to make a stiff dough.
2 Knead in bowl 10 to 15 minutes, or until smooth. Wrap in wax paper or transparent wrap; chill several hours, or until firm. (Overnight is even better.)
3 Roll dough, a rounded teaspoonful at a time, between palms of hands, into 1-inch balls. Place, 2 inches apart, on ungreased large cookie sheets. Flatten with a floured cookie mold or a small glass to a ¼-inch thickness.
4 Bake in slow oven (300°) 25 minutes, or until firm and lightly golden. Remove from cookie sheets to wire racks; cool completely. Attach a small round tip to a cake-decorating set. Fill with DECORATOR'S ICING. Pipe design on cookies, following patterned tops; or glaze entire top with icing. Let stand until design is firm. Store in a tightly covered container.
   DECORATOR'S ICING—Combine 1 cup 10X (confectioners' powdered) sugar, 2½ teaspoons water, and 10 drops yellow food coloring in a small bowl, mixing until smooth. Makes about ⅓ cup icing, or enough for 6 dozen 1½-inch cookies.

Butternuts

Bake at 325° for 15 minutes. Makes about 8 dozen

    ¾ cup (1½ sticks) butter or margarine
    ½ cup sifted 10X (confectioners' powdered) sugar
    ¼ teaspoon salt
    1¾ cups sifted all-purpose flour
    1 package (6 ounces) butterscotch-flavor pieces (1 cup)
    1 cup finely chopped pecans
      RUM GLAZE (recipe follows)
      Pecan halves
      Candied red cherries, halved

1 Cream butter or margarine with 10X sugar and salt in a medium-size bowl; blend in flour until smooth. Stir in butterscotch pieces and pecans.

2 Shape dough, a scant teaspoonful at a time, into balls between palms of hands; place, 1 inch apart, on large ungreased cookie sheets.

3 Bake in slow oven (325°) 15 minutes, or until firm but not brown. Remove from cookie sheets to wire racks; let cool completely.

4 Make RUM GLAZE. Place cookies in a single layer on wire racks set over wax paper; spoon glaze over each to cover completely. (Scrape glaze that drips onto paper back into bowl and beat until smooth before using again.) Decorate each with a pecan or candied-cherry half. Let cookies stand until glaze is firm.

RUM GLAZE—Combine 2 cups sifted 10X (confectioners' powdered) sugar and ¼ cup light rum in a medium-size bowl; beat until smooth. Makes ¾ cup.

Almond Wreaths
Bake at 300° for 20 minutes. Makes about 5 dozen

2 cans (5 ounces each) whole blanched almonds
2 cups sifted all-purpose flour
1 cup (2 sticks) butter or margarine
1 cup 10X (confectioners' powdered) sugar
2 tablespoons lemon juice
Red and green candied cherries

1 Chop or grind almonds very fine; mix with flour in a medium-size bowl.

2 Cream butter or margarine with 10X sugar until fluffy-light in a large bowl; beat in lemon juice.

3 Stir in flour mixture, a third at a time, blending well to make a soft dough. Chill several hours, or overnight, until firm enough to handle.

4 Roll dough, a heaping teaspoonful at a time, into balls between palms of hands. Place, 2 inches apart, on large ungreased cookie sheets.

5 Flatten each ball to a 2-inch round with palm of hand; press a hole in center with tip of wooden-spoon handle. Decorate each with half a red cherry and slivers of green cherry.

6 Bake in slow oven (300°) 20 minutes, or until firm but not brown. Remove carefully from cookie sheets to wire racks; cool completely.

No-Bake Chocolate Truffles
Makes 6 dozen

1 package (6 ounces) semisweet-chocolate pieces
½ cup orange juice
3 tablespoons light rum
1 package (8½ ounces) chocolate wafer cookies, crushed
3 cups sifted 10X (confectioners' powdered) sugar
1 cup very finely chopped walnuts
1 container (4 ounces) chocolate decorating sprinkles
Red candied cherries

1 Melt chocolate pieces in top of a double boiler over simmering water; remove from heat. Blend in orange juice and rum; stir in chocolate cooky crumbs, 2 cups of the 10X sugar, and nuts until well-mixed. Cover; chill about 2 hours, or until stiff enough to handle.

2 Roll dough, a rounded teaspoonful at a time, into balls between palms of hands. Roll balls in chocolate sprinkles to coat generously, pressing firmly as you roll. Place on a tray; cover; chill several hours or overnight.

3 Blend remaining 1 cup 10X sugar with enough water in a small bowl to make a smooth thick glaze. Dip chocolate balls halfway into glaze to coat tops. Decorate with candied cherry pieces; place on wire racks until glaze is set.

Ginger Wafers
Bake at 350° for 13 minutes. Makes about 4 dozen

2 cups sifted all-purpose flour
3 teaspoons ground ginger
2 teaspoons baking soda
1 teaspoon ground cinnamon
½ teaspoon salt
¾ cup (1½ sticks) butter or margarine
1 cup sugar (for dough)
1 egg
¼ cup molasses
Sugar (for coating)

1 Sift flour, ginger, soda, cinnamon, and salt onto wax paper.

2 Cream butter or margarine with the 1 cup sugar until fluffy in a medium-size bowl; beat in egg and molasses.

3 Stir in flour mixture, a third at a time, until well-blended.

4 Roll dough, a teaspoonful at a time, into small balls between palms of hands; roll each in sugar

573

in a pie plate to coat generously. Place, 2 inches apart, on ungreased cookie sheets.

5 Bake in moderate oven (350°) 13 minutes, or until tops are crackled. Remove from cookie sheets to wire racks. Cool completely.

Meltaways
Bake at 350° for 15 minutes. Makes about 3 dozen double cookies

    1 cup (2 sticks) butter or margarine
1½ cups sifted 10X (confectioners' powdered)
        sugar
1½ cups sifted all-purpose flour
    1 teaspoon vanilla
  ¾ cup finely chopped walnuts
    1 can vanilla creamy-type frosting
        Red, yellow, or green food coloring

1 Beat butter or margarine with ½ cup of the 10X sugar until fluffy-light in a large bowl. Stir in flour, vanilla, and nuts, blending well to make a stiff dough.
2 Roll dough, a level teaspoonful at a time, into balls between palms of hands. Place, one inch apart, on lightly greased cookie sheets.
3 Bake in moderate oven (350°) 15 minutes, or until firm. Remove carefully from cookie sheets; while still hot, roll in 10X sugar. Cool on wire racks; roll again in 10X sugar to make a generous white coating.
4 Spoon frosting into a small bowl. Tint pink, green, or yellow with food coloring. Attach a small round tip to a cake-decorating set; fill tube with tinted frosting. Pipe frosting onto flat sides of half the cookies (or spread frosting with a small spatula). Press flat sides of remaining cookies to frosted cookies. Stand cookies on edge on wire racks until frosting is firm. Or divide frosting evenly into 3 small bowls; tint pink, yellow, and green. Fill cake-decorating set with one color at a time, washing set as you change colors.

Swedish Candy Nuggets
Chocolate-candy pieces or bright gumdrops go into the center of each of these crunchy almond cookies.
Bake at 375° for 15 minutes. Makes 3 dozen

  ½ cup (1 stick) butter or margarine
  ¼ cup firmly packed brown sugar
    1 egg, separated
  ½ teaspoon vanilla
    1 cup sifted all-purpose flour
  ¼ teaspoon salt
  ½ cup coarsely chopped almonds
  ¼ cup semisweet-chocolate pieces
  18 small red gumdrops

1 Cream butter or margarine and brown sugar until fluffy in medium-size bowl; beat in egg yolk and vanilla. (Save egg white for next step.) Sift in flour and salt gradually, stirring until well-blended. Chill several hours, or until firm enough to handle.
2 Beat saved egg white with a fork until foamy in pie plate; place almonds in second pie plate.
3 Roll dough, a heaping teaspoonful at a time, into marble-size balls between palms of hands. Roll each in egg white, then in almonds. Place, 3 inches apart, on greased cookie sheets.
4 Make a hollow in center of each ball with tip of finger or handle of wooden spoon. Fill hollows of half with 3 each semisweet-chocolate pieces, pointed ends up; fill each of remaining with a single gumdrop.
5 Bake in moderate oven (375°) 15 minutes, or until firm and lightly golden. Remove carefully from cookie sheets; cool on wire racks. Store in container with tight-fitting cover.

Swedish Sand Tarts
Bake these almond morsels in tiny molds, then dust with sugar and top with jelly.
Bake at 325° for 10 minutes. Makes about 8 dozen

    1 cup (2 sticks) butter or margarine
    1 cup sugar
    1 egg
  ½ teaspoon almond extract
    2 cups sifted all-purpose flour
  ¼ teaspoon salt
  ½ cup sifted 10X (confectioners' powdered)
        sugar
  ¼ cup red currant jelly

1 Cream butter or margarine with sugar until light in medium-size bowl; beat in egg and almond extract. Gradually sift in flour and salt, blending well. Chill dough overnight, or until firm enough to handle.
2 Pinch off about a half teaspoonful at a time and press into ungreased individual sand-tart tins, or miniature fluted tart pans. (Shop for them where fancy imported housewares are sold.) Place on cookie sheet.
3 Bake in slow oven (325°) 10 minutes, or until

Peanuts make marvelous cookies, the nuts themselves or, as in Peanut-Butter Crisscrosses, peanut butter.

lightly golden. Cool in tins until easy to handle, then remove carefully.

4 When ready to serve, dust cookies lightly with 10X sugar; top with a dot of currant jelly.

●

Peanut-Butter Crisscrosses

Orange juice adds a subtle new flavor to these melt-in-your-mouth favorites.
Bake at 375° for 12 minutes. Makes about 5 dozen

  2 cups sifted all-purpose flour
  ¾ teaspoon baking soda
  ½ teaspoon baking powder
  ¼ teaspoon salt
  ½ cup vegetable shortening
  ½ cup peanut butter
  ½ cup firmly packed brown sugar
  ½ cup granulated sugar
  1 egg
  ¼ cup orange juice

1 Measure flour, soda, baking powder, and salt into a sifter.

2 Cream shortening and peanut butter with brown and granulated sugars until fluffy in a large bowl; beat in egg. Sift in flour mixture, adding alternately with orange juice and blending well to make a stiff dough. Chill until firm enough to handle.

3 Roll dough, a teaspoonful at a time, into balls; place, 3 inches apart, on ungreased cookie sheets; flatten, crisscross fashion, with a fork.

4 Bake in moderate oven (375°) 12 minutes, or until golden. Remove from cookie sheets; cool completely on wire racks.

●

Robin's Nests

Bake at 350° for 12 minutes. Makes 3 dozen

  2¼ cups sifted all-purpose flour
  1 cup (2 sticks) butter or margarine
  ½ cup firmly packed brown sugar

2 eggs, separated
1½ teaspoons vanilla
1½ cups finely chopped walnuts
    FONDANT EGGS (recipe follows)

1 Sift flour onto wax paper.
2 Cream butter or margarine with brown sugar until fluffy-light in a medium-size bowl; beat in egg yolks and vanilla. Stir in flour, half at a time, blending well to make a stiff dough.
3 Beat egg whites until foamy in a pie plate; sprinkle walnuts on wax paper.
4 Roll dough, 1 teaspoonful at a time, into balls between palms of hands; roll each in egg white, then into walnuts to coat all over. Place, 2 inches apart, on ungreased large cookie sheets. Press a hollow in center of each with fingertip.
5 Bake in moderate oven (350°) 12 minutes, or until firm and lightly golden. Remove from cookie sheets to wire racks; cool completely. Place a FONDANT EGG in each ''nest.''

FONDANT EGGS—Cream 2 tablespoons butter or margarine until soft in a small bowl; stir in 3 tablespoons light corn syrup, ½ teaspoon almond extract, and 2 cups sifted 10X (confectioners' powdered) sugar until smooth. Knead in 2 drops blue food coloring and 1 drop green food coloring to tint robin's-egg blue. Pinch off fondant, ½ teaspoonful at a time, and roll into egg shapes between palms of hands. Makes 3 dozen tiny candy eggs.

Beau Bows

These crisp shattery curlicues literally melt away in your mouth.
Bake at 350° for 10 minutes. Makes about 5 dozen

½ cup (1 stick) butter or margarine
¼ cup sugar
1 hard-cooked egg yolk
1 raw egg yolk
1¼ cups sifted all-purpose flour
1 egg white, slightly beaten
1 tablespoon cinnamon-sugar

576

1 Cream butter or margarine with sugar until light in medium-size bowl.
2 Press hard-cooked egg yolk through sieve; stir into creamed mixture with raw egg yolk. Gradually sift in flour, blending well. Chill dough overnight, or until firm enough to handle.
3 Pinch off about a half teaspoonful at a time and roll into a very thin straw, about 5 inches

long, on lightly floured pastry cloth or board. Place on lightly greased cookie sheet; shape into a bow by looping ends toward middle; repeat.
4 Brush tops lightly with egg white; sprinkle with cinnamon-sugar.
5 Bake in moderate oven (350°) 10 minutes, or until lightly golden. Remove very carefully from cookie sheets; cool on wire racks. (These are patience-taking cookies, but so worth the effort!)

Star Brights

Bake at 375° for 10 minutes. Makes 6 dozen double cookies

1½ cups (3 sticks) butter or margarine
1 cup sugar
1 egg
1 teaspoon vanilla
¼ teaspoon salt
4½ cups sifted all-purpose flour
½ teaspoon almond extract
    Green food coloring
    Green candied cherries
    Tiny yellow candies

1 Beat butter or margarine with sugar until fluffy-light in a large bowl. Beat in egg, vanilla, and salt. Stir in 4 cups of the flour, a third at a time, blending well to make a soft dough.
2 Divide dough evenly into two bowls. Stir remaining ½ cup flour into one half for making cookie rounds; reserve for Step 4.
3 Blend almond extract and enough green food coloring into remaining half of dough to tint a light green. Chill 30 minutes.
4 Roll plain dough, a teaspoonful at a time, into balls between palms of hands; place 2 inches apart on ungreased cookie sheets. Lightly grease bottom of a drinking glass; dip in granulated sugar; press balls of dough carefully into circles about ⅛ inch thick. Redip glass for each cooky.
5 Fit star plate or disk onto cookie press; fill with green dough; press out onto ungreased cookie sheets. Chill until firm enough to lift without breaking; remove with spatula, placing one green star on each plain sugared round. Decorate with green candied cherries and tiny yellow candies.
6 Bake in moderate oven (375°) 10 minutes, or until firm. Remove from cookie sheets to wire racks; cool completely.

Almond Cuplets

Bake at 350° for 15 minutes. Makes about 4 dozen

1⅓ cups sifted all-purpose flour
¼ teaspoon baking powder
½ cup (1 stick) butter or margarine (for pastry)
2½ cups sifted 10X (confectioners' powdered) sugar
3 eggs
2 tablespoons melted butter or margarine (for filling)
1 cup toasted slivered almonds, ground
1 teaspoon grated lemon rind
2 teaspoons almond extract
Candied red and green cherries

1 Measure flour and baking powder into a sifter.
2 Beat the ½ cup butter or margarine and ½ cup of the 10X sugar until fluffy-light in a medium-size bowl. Sift in flour mixture, a third at a time, blending well; stir in 1 of the eggs to form a stiff dough. Chill several hours, or overnight.
3 Pinch off dough, a teaspoonful at a time, and press over bottoms and sides of 1¾-inch fluted tart-shell pans to make shells. (Or press into tiny muffin-pan cups.)
4 Beat remaining 2 eggs slightly in a medium-size bowl; stir in 1 cup of the remaining 10X sugar, melted butter or margarine, ground almonds, lemon rind, and 1 teaspoon of the almond extract.
5 Spoon 1 teaspoonful of the filling into each pastry-lined pan to fill about halfway. Set pans in a large shallow pan for easy handling.
6 Bake in moderate oven (350°) 15 minutes, or until golden. Cool in pans on a wire rack 10 minutes; remove tarts carefully from pans, easing out with the tip of a small knife, if needed.
7 Beat remaining 1 cup 10X sugar with remaining 1 teaspoon almond extract and a few drops water until smooth in a small bowl. Spread about ½ teaspoonful over each tart to glaze lightly. Garnish with thin slices of red and green cherries.

Peppermint Bonbons

Bake at 350° for 12 minutes. Makes about 4 dozen

2 cups sifted all-purpose flour
½ teaspoon baking powder
½ teaspoon salt
½ cup (1 stick) butter or margarine
½ cup sugar
1 egg

1 square unsweetened chocolate, melted
1 teaspoon vanilla
PEPPERMINT GLAZE (recipe follows)

1 Sift flour, baking powder, and salt onto wax paper.
2 Cream butter or margarine with sugar until fluffy-light in a large bowl; beat in egg, chocolate, and vanilla. Stir in flour mixture, half at a time, blending well to make a stiff dough.
3 Roll dough, a rounded teaspoonful at a time, into balls between palms of hands; place, 1 inch apart, on lightly greased large cookie sheets.
4 Bake in moderate oven (350°) 12 minutes, or until firm. Remove from cookie sheets to wire racks; let cool completely.
5 When ready to frost cookies, place about an inch apart on wire racks set on wax paper or foil. Spoon PEPPERMINT GLAZE over cookies to cover completely; let set slightly. Scrape any frosting that drips onto paper back into bowl; stir well. Spoon another layer over cookies to make a thick coating; let stand until firm. Trim with holly leaves and berries, using decorating frostings in pressurized cans or plastic tubes, if you wish.

PEPPERMINT GLAZE—Combine 3 cups sifted 10X (confectioners' powdered) sugar, 3 tablespoons water, ¼ teaspoon peppermint extract, and ¼ teaspoon red food coloring in a medium-size bowl; beat until smooth. (Frosting will be thin enough to pour from a spoon. If it gets too thick while frosting cookies, add a few drops water and beat again until smooth.) Makes about 1 cup.

Tangerine Snowballs

Makes about 3½ dozen

1 package (10 ounces) shortbread cookies, crushed
1 cup flaked coconut
⅔ cup sifted 10X (confectioners' powdered) sugar (for cookies)
½ cup thawed frozen concentrate for tangerine juice
Sifted 10X (confectioners' powdered) sugar (for coating)

1 Mix cookie crumbs, coconut, and the ⅔ cup 10X sugar in a medium-size bowl.
2 Stir in tangerine juice until well-blended.
3 Roll mixture, a teaspoonful at a time, into balls

577

between palms of hands; roll each in 10X sugar in a pie plate to coat generously.

Sesame Wafers
Bake at 350° for 10 minutes. Makes 8 dozen

> 2 cups sifted all-purpose flour
> ½ teaspoon baking soda
> ½ teaspoon salt
> 1 cup (2 sticks) butter or margarine
> 1 cup sugar
> 1 egg
> 1 teaspoon vanilla
> 2 packages (about 2 ounces each) sesame
>   seeds (about ½ cup)

1 Sift flour, soda, and salt onto wax paper.
2 Cream butter or margarine with sugar until fluffy-light in a large bowl; beat in egg and vanilla.
3 Stir in flour mixture, half at a time, blending well to make a soft dough. Chill several hours, or overnight, until firm enough to handle.
4 Roll dough, a teaspoonful at a time, into balls between palms of hands, then roll in sesame seeds in a pie plate to coat lightly. Place, 2 inches apart, on lightly greased large cookie sheets.
5 Bake in moderate oven (350°) 10 minutes, or until delicately golden. Remove from cookie sheets to wire racks; cool completely.

Viennese Rounds
Double-deck cookies with raspberry filling inspired by the famous Linzer torte.
Bake at 350° for 10 minutes. Makes about 3 dozen double cookies

> 1 cup (2 sticks) butter or margarine
> 1½ cups sifted 10X (confectioners' powdered)
>   sugar
> 1½ cups sifted all-purpose flour
> 1 teaspoon vanilla
> ½ cup filberts or hazelnuts, ground
>   Red food coloring
> 1 cup red raspberry preserves

1 Cream butter or margarine and ½ cup of the 10X sugar until well-blended in a large bowl; stir in flour, vanilla, and ground nuts.
2 Roll dough, a level teaspoonful at a time, into balls between palms of hands. Place, 2 inches

apart, on greased cookie sheets. Lightly grease the bottom of a measuring cup and dip in 10X sugar; press over each ball to flatten to an about-1-inch round.
3 Bake in moderate oven (350°) 10 minutes, or until golden around edges. Remove carefully from cookie sheets to wire racks; cool completely.
4 Beat remaining 1 cup 10X sugar with a few drops water until smooth in a small bowl; tint pink with a drop or two food coloring.
5 Spread bottoms of half of the cookies with raspberry preserves; top, sandwich style, with remaining cookies, flat side down.
6 Attach a writing tip to a cake-decorating set; fill decorator with pink frosting; press out in rings on tops of cookies.

Pfeffernuss Drops
These sugar dainties have all the spicy flavor of the old-fashioned German kind.
Bake at 350° for 8 minutes. Makes about 6 dozen

> 1¾ cups sifted all-purpose flour
> 1 teaspoon ground cinnamon
> ¼ teaspoon baking soda
> ¼ teaspoon salt
> ¼ teaspoon ground nutmeg
> ⅛ teaspoon ground cloves
> ⅛ teaspoon pepper
> ½ teaspoon anise seeds
> ½ teaspoon crushed cardamom seeds (from
>   10 pods)
> ¼ cup candied citron, finely chopped
> ¼ cup candied orange peel, finely chopped
> 2 tablespoons butter or margarine
> 1¼ cups sifted 10X (confectioners' powdered)
>   sugar
> 1 egg
>   Red and green candied cherries
> 1 teaspoon milk

1 Sift first seven ingredients into large bowl; stir in anise seeds, cardamom seeds, citron, and orange peel.
2 Cream butter or margarine and 1 cup 10X sugar until well-mixed in medium-size bowl. (Save remaining ¼ cup for Step 4.) Gradually stir in egg, then flour mixture, just until blended. Chill overnight, or until firm enough to handle.

3 Roll dough, about 1 teaspoonful at a time, into small balls; place, 2 inches apart, on greased cookie sheets. Top each with a piece of candied cherry.
4 Stir milk into saved ¼ cup 10X sugar until smooth in small cup. Drizzle very lightly over top of each cooky.
5 Bake in moderate oven (350°) 8 minutes, or until very lightly browned. Remove from cookie sheets at once; cool on wire racks.

Candy Canes
Bake at 350° for 12 minutes. Makes 2½ dozen

  2 cups sifted all-purpose flour
  ½ teaspoon baking soda
  ¼ teaspoon salt
  ⅔ cup butter or margarine
  ⅔ cup sugar
  1 whole egg
  1 egg yolk
  1 teaspoon vanilla
    ORNAMENTAL FROSTING (see index for recipe page number)
    Red food coloring

1 Sift flour, soda, and salt onto wax paper.
2 Cream butter or margarine with sugar until fluffy-light in a large bowl; beat in egg, egg yolk, and vanilla. Stir in flour mixture, half at a time, blending well to make a stiff dough.
3 Roll out dough, an eighth at a time, on a lightly floured pastry cloth or board with palms of hands to a log about as thick as a pencil. Cut into 5-inch lengths. Place, 1 inch apart, on lightly greased large cookie sheets. Curve one end of each to resemble a cane.
4 Bake in moderate oven (350°) 12 minutes, or until firm and lightly golden. Remove from cookie sheets to wire racks; cool completely.
5 Frost canes with part of the ORNAMENTAL FROSTING. Stir a few drops red food coloring into remaining frosting to tint deep pink; press through a cake-decorating set onto frosted canes to form stripes. Let stand on wire racks until frosting is firm.

Candy-Stripe Twists
These fun-to-make cookies taste like old-fashioned licorice sticks.
Bake at 350° for 10 minutes. Makes 5 dozen

  3¼ cups sifted all-purpose flour
  4 teaspoons baking powder
  1 teaspoon salt
  ½ cup (1 stick) butter or margarine
  1¼ cups sugar
  1 egg
  ½ teaspoon oil of anise
  ¼ cup milk
    Red food coloring

1 Measure flour, baking powder, and salt into sifter.
2 Cream butter or margarine and sugar until fluffy in large bowl; beat in egg and oil of anise.
3 Sift in dry ingredients, a third at a time, adding alternately with milk; stir until well-blended.
4 Spoon half of dough into a medium-size bowl; blend in a few drops red food coloring to tint pink; leave other half plain.
5 Pinch off about a teaspoonful each of pink and white doughs at a time, and roll each into a pencil-thin strip about 5 inches long on lightly floured pastry cloth or board. Place strips side by side, pressing ends together, then twist into a rope. Place, 1 inch apart, on ungreased cookie sheets.
6 Bake in moderate oven (350°) 10 minutes, or until firm. Remove carefully from cookie sheets; cool on wire racks. Store, with wax paper or transparent wrap between layers, in container with tight-fitting cover.

Chocolate-Almond Snowdrops
Each of these little sugar-coated treats disappears in about two bites.
Bakes at 325° for 20 minutes. Makes 4 dozen

  ½ cup (1 stick) butter or margarine
  3 tablespoons 10X (confectioners' powdered) sugar
  ⅔ cup sifted all-purpose flour
  ⅓ cup dry cocoa mix
  1 cup finely chopped almonds
    10X (confectioners' powdered) sugar

579

1 Cream butter or margarine with the 3 tablespoons 10X sugar until fluffy in a medium-size bowl; stir in flour and cocoa mix, then almonds. Chill until firm enough to handle.
2 Roll dough, a teaspoonful at a time, into marble-size balls; place, 2 inches apart, on ungreased cookie sheets.
3 Bake in slow oven (325°) 20 minutes, or until firm. Remove carefully from cookie sheets; while still warm, roll in 10X sugar to coat generously; cool completely on wire racks.

Peppernut Bonbons

These spicy dainties are so tiny that more than 2 dozen fit into a teacup.
Bake at 350° for 10 to 12 minutes. Makes about 12 dozen tiny balls or about 5 dozen 1-inch balls

2 cups sifted all-purpose flour
1 teaspoon baking powder
⅛ teaspoon salt
¼ teaspoon ground cinnamon
⅛ teaspoon ground nutmeg
⅛ teaspoon pepper
　Dash of ground cloves
¼ teaspoon anise seeds
⅛ teaspoon crushed cardamom seeds (from 3 pods)
¼ cup candied citron, finely chopped
¼ cup blanched almonds, finely chopped
4 tablespoons (½ stick) butter or margarine
½ cup sugar
1 egg
½ teaspoon grated lemon rind
1 teaspoon lemon juice
　LEMON FONDANT FROSTING (recipe follows)
　Red and green candied cherries, cut in tiny pieces

1 Sift flour, baking powder, salt, cinnamon, nutmeg, pepper, and cloves into a small bowl. Stir in anise and cardamom seeds, citron, and almonds.
2 Cream butter or margarine with sugar until fluffy in a large bowl; beat in egg and lemon rind and juice.
3 Stir in flour mixture, half at a time, blending well to make a stiff dough. Wrap in wax paper or transparent wrap; chill several hours, or until firm enough to handle. (Overnight is even better.)
4 Roll dough, a rounded ½ teaspoonful at a time for tiny balls, or a rounded teaspoonful for larger ones, into balls between palms of hands; place, 1 inch apart, on lightly greased cookie sheets.
5 Bake in moderate oven (350°) 10 minutes for small balls, and 12 minutes for larger ones, or until firm but not brown. Remove from cookie sheets; cool completely on wire racks. Store in tightly covered containers until ready to frost and decorate just before serving or giving.
6 To frost and decorate, place about 1 dozen tiny balls at a time, 2 inches apart, on wax paper or foil. (Larger balls can be set on a wire rack with wax paper or foil underneath to catch excess frosting.) Spoon LEMON FONDANT FROST-ING over balls to cover completely; let set slightly; top with pieces of red and green cherries for holly berries and leaves. (Job is easier if you use tweezers to set decorations in place.)
7 Lift tiny balls onto clean wax paper or foil;

let stand until frosting is firm. (Leave larger balls on racks until frosting sets.) Scrape any frosting that drips onto wax paper or foil back into bowl; stir well. Frost and decorate remaining balls.

Lemon Fondant Frosting

It couldn't be easier, for it's the no-cook kind—and a perfect keeper if stored in a covered jar in the refrigerator.
Makes about ¾ cup

2 cups 10X (confectioners' powdered) sugar
2 tablespoons water
1½ teaspoon lemon juice
　Yellow and green food colorings

1 Mix 10X sugar with water and lemon juice in a medium-size bowl; beat until smooth.
2 Tint lightly with a drop each of yellow and green food colorings. (Frosting will be just thick enough to pour from a spoon. If it gets too thick while frosting cookies, add a drop or two of water and beat again until smooth. If made ahead, remove from refrigerator about an hour before frosting cookies to soften.)

COOKIE PRESS COOKIES

Spritz Cookies

This is a traditional Christmas cookie—so rich, so good.
Bake at 400° about 10 minutes. Makes about 12 dozen small cookies

2 cups (1 pound) butter or margarine (or use part shortening)
2 cups sugar
4 egg yolks
1 teaspoon vanilla
5 cups sifted all-purpose flour
　Nuts
　Candied cherries
　Tinted sugars
　Silver candies
　CREAMY FROSTING (recipe follows)
　Melted chocolate

1 Cream butter or margarine until soft in large bowl; gradually add sugar, creaming well after each addition until light and fluffy.

Up, up and away—a balloon full of spritz cookies.

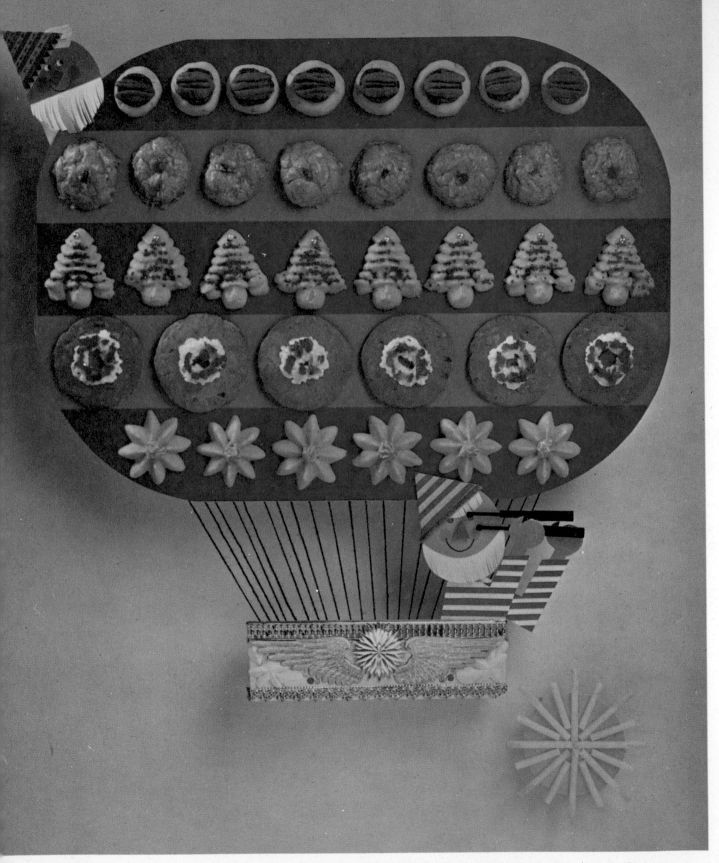

More cookie press cookies (bottom and center rows), the dough tinted palest, palest green for Christmas.

2 Add egg yolks, one at a time, beating well after each addition; stir in vanilla, then flour, a small amount at a time; mix well.

3 Pack dough into metal cookie press; press out dough into Christmas trees, bars, stars, and other fancy shapes onto ungreased cookie sheets; decorate some with halved nuts, candied cherries, tinted sugar, and/or silver candies; leave others plain, to frost after baking.

4 Bake in hot oven (400°) 10 minutes, or until edges are golden.

5 Remove from cookie sheets with spatula; cool on wire cake racks.

6 Frost plain tops with colored CREAMY FROSTING and decorate with tinted sugar and silver candies; dip ends of bar-shape cookies in melted chocolate.

CREAMY FROSTING—Beat 2 egg whites, ¼ teaspoon cream of tartar, and ¼ teaspoon vanilla until foamy in medium-size bowl; gradually beat in 2½ cups sifted 10X (confectioners' powdered) sugar until frosting stands in firm peaks. Divide among custard cups; leave one white and tint others with food colorings. (If frosting gets too firm to work with easily, stir in a drop or two of hot water.)

●

Spritz Slims
Bake at 375° for 8 minutes. Makes 12 dozen

    1½ cups (3 sticks) butter or margarine
     1 cup sugar
     3 egg yolks
     1 teaspoon vanilla
     ¼ teaspoon salt
    3½ cups sifted all-purpose flour
     4 squares (4 ounces) semisweet chocolate
     1 tablespoon vegetable shortening
    ⅔ cup chopped pistachio nuts

1 Beat butter or margarine with sugar until fluffy-light in a large bowl. Beat in egg yolks, vanilla, and salt. Stir in flour, a third at a time, blending well to make a soft dough.

2 Fit rosette plate or star disk onto cookie press; fill press with dough (or fit pastry bag with a small star tip). Press dough out into 3-inch lengths on ungreased large cookie sheets.

3 Bake in moderate oven (375°) 8 minutes, or until firm; remove from cookie sheets to wire racks; cool completely.

4 Melt semisweet chocolate with shortening in top of double boiler; cool.

5 Dip ends of slims into melted chocolate, then into chopped nuts. Place on wire racks until decoration is firm.

To make CHOCOLATE SUNBURSTS: Prepare SPRITZ SLIMS dough, adding 4 squares melted and cooled unsweetened chocolate with the butter or margarine. Place dough in a cookie press fitted with a sunburst plate or disk; press out onto ungreased cookie sheets. Bake and cool as above. Decorate with frosting from a pressurized can, if you wish.

Entwined rings fashioned with the cookie press.

Almond-Butter Cookies
A traditional rich dough to squeeze through a cookie press into varied shapes; six are given here.
Bake at 350° for 12 to 15 minutes. Makes 7 to 8 dozen

    1 can (about 5 ounces) blanched almonds
    1 cup (2 sticks) butter or margarine
    ¾ cup sugar
    2 eggs
    1 teaspoon vanilla
    1 teaspoon almond extract
    2½ cups sifted all-purpose flour
    1 recipe ORNAMENTAL FROSTING (see index for recipe page number)

1 Put almonds through food chopper, using fine blade, or chop finely in an electric blender.

2 Cream butter or margarine with sugar until light in large bowl; beat in eggs, vanilla, and almond extract. Stir in ground almonds; gradually sift in flour, blending well, to make a soft dough.

3 Divide evenly into 6 small bowls. Flavor, shape, and decorate each variety, following recipes below.

4 Bake all cookies in moderate oven (350°) 12 to 15 minutes, or until firm. Remove from cookie sheets; cool completely on wire racks, then decorate.

Frosted Snowflakes: Fit snowflake or star plate or disk on cookie press. Fill with dough from one bowl and press out on ungreased cookie sheets. Bake and cool, following directions for ALMOND-BUTTER COOKIES. Decorate centers with a swirl of plain ORNAMENTAL FROSTING; sprinkle tops lightly with dry cocoa.

Christmas Canes: Fit star plate or disk on cookie press. Fill with dough from second bowl and press out into 5-inch lengths on ungreased cookie sheets; turn one end to form a crook.

583

Bake and cool, following directions for AL-MOND-BUTTER COOKIES. Tint a small amount OR-NAMENTAL FROSTING pale green with a few drops green food coloring. Decorate canes with frosting stripes; top with multicolor sprinkles.

Brown-Eyed Susans: Fit sunburst or star plate or disk on cookie press. Fill with dough from third bowl and press out on ungreased cookie sheets. Bake and cool, following directions for ALMOND-BUTTER COOKIES. Tint a small amount ORNAMENTAL FROSTING yellow with a few drops yellow food coloring. Decorate centers of cookies with a tiny swirl; top with semisweet-chocolate pieces.

Party Wreaths: Fit star plate or disk on cookie press. Fill with dough from fourth bowl and press out into 3-inch lengths on ungreased cookie sheets; join ends together to form a circle. Bake and cool, following directions for ALMOND-BUTTER COOKIES. Tint a small amount ORNAMENTAL FROSTING pale green with a few drops green food coloring. Decorate wreaths with a frosting swirl; sprinkle with red decorating sugar.

Green Trees and **Holiday Daisies:** Combine dough in remaining 2 bowls. Tint green with a few drops green food coloring. For **Green Trees,** fit tree plate or disk on cookie press. Fill with dough and press out on ungreased cookie sheets. Sprinkle with red decorating sugar; top each with a silver candy. For **Holiday Daisies,** fit sunburst or star plate or disk on cookie press. Fill with dough and press out on ungreased cookie sheets. Bake and cool both, following directions for ALMOND-BUTTER COOKIES. To decorate **Holiday Daisies,** tint a small amount OR-NAMENTAL FROSTING pink with a few drops red food coloring; flavor, if you wish, with a drop or two of peppermint extract. Swirl in center of cookies.

Wreaths
Bake at 350° for 12 minutes. Makes 6 dozen

    1 cup (2 sticks) butter or margarine
    ½ cup sugar
    1 egg
    1 teaspoon vanilla
    2½ cups sifted all-purpose flour
    1⅓ cups finely chopped walnuts
    ¼ cup maple syrup
      Red and green candied cherries

1 Beat butter or margarine with sugar until fluffy-light in a large bowl. Beat in egg and vanilla. Stir in flour, a third at a time, blending well to make a soft dough.

2 Measure out ⅓ cup of the dough and mix with walnuts and maple syrup in a small bowl; reserve for cookie centers in Step 3.

3 Fit a pastry bag with a small star tip; fill bag with remaining dough. Press out into 1½-inch rings on ungreased large cookie sheets; fill center of each cookie with about a teaspoonful of nut mixture; decorate wreaths with slivers of red and green candied cherries.

4 Bake in moderate oven (350°) 12 minutes, or until lightly golden at edges. Remove carefully from cookie sheets to wire racks; cool completely.

Fruit Spritz
Bake at 375° for 10 minutes. Makes about 10 dozen

    4½ cups sifted all-purpose flour
    1 teaspoon baking powder
      Dash of salt
    1½ cups (3 sticks) butter or margarine
    1 cup sugar
    1 egg
    2 tablespoons thawed frozen concentrate for
      pineapple-orange juice
      Silver decorating candies
      Red and green decorating sugars

1 Sift flour, baking powder, and salt onto wax paper.

2 Cream butter or margarine with sugar until fluffy-light in a large bowl; beat in egg and pineapple-orange juice.

3 Stir in flour mixture, a quarter at a time, blending well to make a stiff dough.

4 Fit rosette, tree, or animal plate or disk onto cookie press; fill with dough. Press out, 1 inch apart, onto large ungreased cookie sheets. Decorate with silver candies or sprinkle with decorating sugars.

584

5 Bake in moderate oven (375°) 10 minutes, or until firm but not brown. Remove from cookie sheets to wire racks; cool completely.

●

Cherry Macaroon Puffs
Egg-white-light and chewy, with a tantalizing taste of almond
Bake at 300° for 20 minutes. Makes about 4 dozen.

1 can (8 ounces) almond paste (not almond paste filling)
3 cups sifted 10X (confectioners' powdered) sugar
2 egg whites
1 teaspoon vanilla
Red and green candied cherries, halved

1 Line 2 large cookie sheets with brown paper.
2 Blend almond paste and 10X sugar thoroughly in a large bowl; beat in unbeaten egg whites and vanilla until smooth.
3 Fit a star tip onto a pastry bag; spoon dough into bag. Press out into star shapes, 1 inch apart, on brown paper. (If you do not have a pastry bag, drop dough by teaspoonfuls onto

Perfect Christmas gifts, when packed in apothecary jars and tied with ribbon: Wreaths (a spritz cookie) and easy-to-shape and bake Candy-Stripe Twists.

Pinwheel cookies are made by sandwiching two doughs together, rolling up, chilling and slicing thin.

paper-lined cookie sheets.) Press half a candied cherry on top of each.

4 Bake in slow oven (300°) 20 minutes, or until lightly golden. Cool on cookie sheets on wire racks; remove cookies carefully from brown paper with a spatula.

Meringue Stars and Kisses

Bake at 250° for 30 minutes. Makes about 5 dozen tiny cookies

2 egg whites
½ teaspoon cream of tartar
⅛ teaspoon salt
  Green food coloring
½ cup granulated sugar
  Green decorating sugar

1 Beat egg whites, cream of tartar, salt, and a few drops green food coloring until foamy-white and double in volume in a medium-size bowl.

2 Sprinkle in granulated sugar, 1 tablespoon at a time, beating all the time until sugar completely dissolves and meringue stands in firm peaks. Beating will take about 10 minutes in all with an electric beater. (If you prefer white cookies, omit food coloring.)

3 Attach a plain or star tip to a pastry bag; spoon meringue into bag. Press out into kisses or stars, 1 inch apart, onto foil-covered large cookie sheets. Leave plain or sprinkle with green sugar.

4 Bake in very slow oven (250°) 30 minutes, or until firm but not brown. Remove carefully from foil to wire racks; cool completely.

586

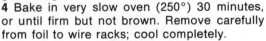

Minted Meringue Trees

Peppermint dainties made with a pastry bag, decorated with candies.
Bake at 225° for 1 hour and 15 minutes. Makes about 3 dozen

2 egg whites
¼ teaspoon cream of tartar
⅛ teaspoon salt
½ cup sugar
¼ teaspoon peppermint extract
¼ teaspoon green food coloring
  Gold, silver, or colored decorating candies

1 Grease cookie sheets; dust lightly with flour.

2 Beat egg whites with cream of tartar and salt until foamy-white and double in volume in a medium-size bowl. Beat in sugar, 1 tablespoon at a time, beating all the time until sugar dissolves completely and meringue stands in firm peaks. Stir in peppermint extract and food coloring.

3 Fit a small star tip onto a pastry bag; spoon meringue into bag. Press out onto cookie sheets in tiny tree shapes, 1 inch apart, swirling meringue into a round at base and building up to a point. Sprinkle with decorating candies.

4 Bake in very slow oven (225°) 1 hour and 15 minutes, or until firm. (Meringues should not brown.) Cool 10 minutes on cookie sheets on wire racks; remove carefully to racks; cool completely.

Meringue Creams

Each little coffee-flavor shell is about as big as a half dollar and holds a billowy party-pink filling.
Bake at 250° for 1 hour. Makes 4 dozen

2 egg whites
1 teaspoon lemon juice
½ cup sugar (for meringue shells)
1 teaspoon vanilla
1 teaspoon instant coffee powder
1 cup cream for whipping
2 tablespoons sugar (for filling)
1 teaspoon brandy flavoring or extract
  Red food coloring

1 Line two large cookie sheets with brown paper; draw 24 one-and-one-half-inch rounds, 2 inches apart, on each paper.

2 Beat egg whites with lemon juice until foamy-white and double in volume in a small bowl. Sprinkle in the ½ cup sugar, 1 tablespoon at a time, beating all the time until sugar completely dissolves and meringue stands in firm peaks; beat in vanilla and instant coffee.

How to have fun at Christmas (or any) time: make up big batches of basic doughs, let everyone pitch in.

3 Attach a fancy tip to a pastry bag; fill bag with meringue. Starting at center of each circle on paper, press out meringue to form tiny shells. (If you do not have a pastry bag, spread 1 tablespoonful meringue into each circle, building up edge slightly.)

4 Bake in very slow oven (250°) 1 hour, or until delicately golden. Cool on cookie sheets 5 minutes; loosen carefully from paper with a spatula; cool completely on wire racks. (If shells are made ahead, place in a single layer in a large shallow pan and store in a cool, dry place.)

5 About an hour before serving, beat cream with the 2 tablespoons sugar until stiff in a medium-size bowl; stir in brandy flavoring or extract and a few drops red food coloring to tint pink. Spoon about 2 teaspoonfuls into each

meringue shell, swirling top to a peak; garnish with a Brazil-nut curl. Chill until serving time. (To make Brazil-nut curls: Cover shelled nuts with boiling water; let stand 5 minutes; drain. While nuts are still warm, shave lengthwise into thin strips with a vegetable parer.)

587

Whirling Stars
Bake at 400° for 10 to 12 minutes. Makes about 5 dozen small cookies

1½ cups (3 sticks) butter or margarine
1 cup sugar
1 egg
1 teaspoon grated lemon rind
1 tablespoon lemon juice

4 cups sifted all-purpose flour
1 teaspoon baking powder
    Silver candies

1 Cream butter or margarine until soft in large bowl; gradually add sugar, creaming well after each addition, until mixture is fluffy.
2 Beat in egg, then lemon rind and juice; blend in flour sifted with baking powder to make a soft dough.
3 Fill metal cookie press with dough; press out into rosettes on ungreased cold cookie sheets; press a silver candy into center of each.
4 Bake in hot oven (400°) 10 to 12 minutes, or until edges are browned.
5 Remove from cookie sheets with spatula; cool on wire cake racks.

COOKIE CUT-OUTS

Tree Frosties
Bake at 350° for 10 minutes. Makes about 4 dozen

1¼ cups sifted all-purpose flour
  ⅓ cup granulated sugar
  ¾ cup (1½ sticks) butter or margarine
  1 egg, separated
  1 cup sifted 10X (confectioners' powdered) sugar
  1 package creamy white frosting mix
    Green and red food coloring

1 Sift flour with granulated sugar into a medium-size bowl.
2 Cut in ½ cup of the butter or margarine with a pastry blender until mixture is crumbly; mix in egg yolk, then knead until mixture forms a stiff dough. Reserve egg white for frosting in Step 4. Wrap dough in wax paper or transparent wrap; chill several hours, or until firm enough to roll. (Overnight is even better.)
3 Cut off one third of the dough; keep remainder chilled. Roll out to a 12½x6-inch rectangle, on a lightly floured pastry cloth or board; trim edges evenly. Cut in half lengthwise, then cut into triangles about 2½ inches wide with a pastry wheel or knife; leave cut-outs in place until frosted. .
4 Mix egg white and 10X sugar until smooth in a small bowl; spread about a third in a thin layer over cut dough. Lift each triangle carefully with a wide spatula and place, 1 inch apart, on a greased large cookie sheet. Roll, cut, and frost each remaining third of dough the same way.

5 Bake in moderate oven (350°) 10 minutes, or until frosting is lightly golden. Remove from cookie sheets; cool completely on wire racks.
6 Prepare frosting mix for decorating with remaining ¼ cup of the butter or margarine and water, following label directions. Tint green and pink with food coloring. Decorate cookies as desired. Let stand until colored frosting is firm.

●

Lebkuchen
Bake at 350° for 10 minutes. Makes about 5 dozen

  ¾ cup honey
  ¾ cup firmly packed dark brown sugar
  1 egg
  2 teaspoons grated lemon rind
  3 tablespoons lemon juice
3½ cups sifted all-purpose flour
  1 teaspoon salt
  1 teaspoon ground cinnamon
  1 teaspoon ground nutmeg
  ½ teaspoon ground allspice
  ½ teaspoon ground ginger
  ¼ teaspoon ground cloves
  ½ teaspoon baking soda
  1 container (8 ounces) citron, finely chopped
  1 cup chopped unblanched almonds
    SUGAR GLAZE (recipe follows)

1 Heat honey to boiling in a small saucepan; pour into a large bowl; cool about 30 minutes.
2 Stir in brown sugar, egg, lemon rind, and lemon juice, blending well.
3 Sift flour, salt, cinnamon, nutmeg, allspice, ginger, cloves, and baking soda onto wax paper.
4 Stir flour mixture into honey mixture a third at a time. Stir in citron and almonds. Dough will be stiff but sticky. Wrap in foil or transparent wrap; chill several hours, or until firm.
5 Roll out dough, ⅛ at a time, on lightly floured pastry cloth or board, to a 6x5-inch rectangle. Cut into 8 rectangles, 2½x1½. Place 1 inch apart on greased large cookie sheets.
6 Bake in moderate oven (350°) for ten minutes, or until firm. Remove to wire racks.
7 While cookies are hot, brush with hot SUGAR GLAZE, then press on a Christmas cut-out. Cool cookies completely before storing. Store in a tightly covered container at least 2 weeks to mellow.
  SUGAR GLAZE—Combine 1½ cups granulated sugar and ¾ cup water in a medium-size saucepan. Bring to boiling; reduce heat; simmer 3

You don't have to have cookie cutters for cut-outs. Make cardboard patterns, cut 'round them with knives. ➤

minutes. Remove from heat; stir in ½ cup sifted 10X (confectioners' powdered) sugar. Makes about 2 cups.

●

Two-in-One Christmas Cut-Out Cookies
Bake at 350° for 8 minutes. Makes about 4 dozen

    4 cups sifted all-purpose flour
    4 teaspoons baking powder
    ½ teaspoon salt
    ⅓ cup butter or margarine
    ⅓ cup firmly packed light brown sugar
    ⅔ cup light molasses
    1 egg
    1 teaspoon vanilla
    ORNAMENTAL FROSTING (see index for recipe
    page number)

Teddy Bear Cookies
(dark dough)

1 Sift flour, baking powder, and salt onto wax paper.
2 Beat butter or margarine with brown sugar until fluffy-light in a medium-size bowl; beat in molasses, egg, and vanilla.
3 Stir in flour mixture, a third at a time, blending well to make a stiff dough. Chill 1 hour, or until firm enough to roll.
4 Roll out dough, one quarter at a time, ⅛ inch thick on lightly floured pastry cloth or board; cut into Teddy Bear shapes with a floured cookie cutter. Place, 1 inch apart, on greased large cookie sheets.
5 Bake in moderate oven (350°) 8 minutes, or until firm. Remove from cookie sheets to wire racks; cool completely.
6 Make ORNAMENTAL FROSTING. Fit a small round tip onto a cake-decorating set; fill tube with frosting. Pipe decorations on cookies. Let stand until frosting is firm.

Christmas Ornament Cookies
(light dough)

Substitute ⅔ cup honey for the molasses and 1 teaspoon lemon extract for the vanilla in above recipe. Roll out dough; cut into Christmas ornament shapes with a floured cookie cutter, or make your own cardboard pattern, cutting out dough around pattern with a sharp knife. Bake and cool, following directions for TEDDY BEAR COOKIES. Brush tops of cookies lightly with corn syrup in a Christmas ornament design; then sprinkle with colored sugars. Let stand until designs are set.

590

The results of a children's cookie cut-out jamboree.

COOKIE JAR JEWELS

Sugar Cookie Cut-Outs

Bake at 350° for 10 minutes. Makes about 5 dozen

3¼ cups sifted all-purpose flour
1 teaspoon baking powder
½ teaspoon salt
¾ cup (1½ sticks) butter or margarine
1 cup sugar
2 eggs
1 teaspoon vanilla
ORNAMENTAL FROSTING *(see index for recipe page number)*

Blue Bells

1 Sift flour, baking powder, and salt onto wax paper.
2 Beat butter or margarine with sugar until fluffy-light in a large bowl. Beat in eggs and vanilla. Stir in flour mixture, a third at a time, blending well to make a stiff dough. Chill several hours or overnight, until firm enough to roll.
3 Roll out dough, one quarter at a time, ⅛ inch thick, on a lightly floured pastry cloth or board; cut into bell shapes with a floured cookie cutter. Place, 1 inch apart, on large cookie sheets. Reroll and cut out all trimmings.
4 Bake in moderate oven (350°) 10 minutes, or until firm and lightly golden. Remove from cookie sheets to wire racks; cool completely.
5 Make ORNAMENTAL FROSTING. Tint ½ cup of the frosting a pale blue with a few drops of blue food coloring in a small bowl. Stir in 2 tablespoons water to make a thin glaze. Dip tops of cookies in glaze; turn right side up; let stand until set. Fit a small round tip onto a cake-decorating set. Fill tube with remaining frosting. Pipe a white outline and small bow on each glazed cookie.

Mexican Chocolate Horses

Prepare SUGAR COOKIE CUTOUT dough, adding 2 envelopes (1 ounce each) liquid unsweetened chocolate with the eggs and vanilla in Step 2. Roll out dough; cut into horse shapes with a floured 2½-inch cookie cutter. Place 1 inch apart on lightly greased large cookie sheets. Bake and cool, following BLUE BELLS' directions

One of the crispiest, loveliest cut-out cookies is the classic Sugar Cookie, rolled thin and baked to perfection.

Everything the cookie artist needs: decorator sugars, dragées, nuts, aromatic seeds, even candied flowers.

above. Make ORNAMENTAL FROSTING. Divide evenly into 4 small bowls. Tint deep pink, orange, and yellow with a few drops of food coloring. Fit tip onto a cake-decorating set. Fill tube with remaining white frosting. Pipe outline of white around horse. Pipe stripes of colored frosting on sides of horse to resemble a striped Mexican blanket, washing decorating set as you change colors. Let stand until frosting is firm.

Springerle
Preheat to 375°. Bake at 300° for 15 minutes. Makes about 6 dozen cookies

    4 eggs
    2 cups sugar
    1 teaspoon anise extract
4¼ cups sifted all-purpose flour
    1 teaspoon baking soda
      Anise seeds

1 Beat eggs in large bowl of electric mixer until very thick (this takes about 10 minutes); gradually add sugar, continuing to beat 15 minutes, or until very light and fluffy.

2 Beat in anise extract, then add flour and baking soda to make a stiff dough.

3 Roll out dough, one quarter at a time, on a lightly floured pastry cloth or board, to ½-inch thickness. Then, using springerle rolling pin, roll over dough only once, pressing designs into dough to a ¼-inch thickness. Cut cookies apart on dividing lines.

4 Grease large cookie sheets; sprinkle lightly with anise seeds. Carefully place cookies, 1 inch apart, on prepared cookie sheets. Let stand 24 hours, uncovered, in cool place (not refrigerator.) Cookies will appear to have white frosting.

5 Place cookies in moderate oven (375°) and immediately reduce heat to slow (300°). Bake 15 minutes, or until set but not browned.

6 Remove cookies to wire racks; cool completely. Store in tightly covered container about 2 weeks to season.

Molasses Midgets
These happy little fellows will charm the children! Cookies are thin, crisp, and rich with molasses.

593

Bake at 350° for 6 minutes. Makes about 6 dozen tiny cookies

1 cup sifted all-purpose flour
½ teaspoon pumpkin-pie spice
¼ teaspoon baking soda
  Dash of salt
2 tablespoons butter or margarine
2 tablespoons brown sugar
¼ cup molasses
  Currants

1 Measure flour, pumpkin-pie spice, soda, and salt into sifter.
2 Cream butter or margarine with brown sugar until fluffy in a medium-size bowl; beat in molasses.
3 Sift in flour mixture, a third at a time, blending well to make a stiff dough. Wrap in wax paper or transparent wrap; chill several hours, or until firm enough to roll. (Overnight is best.)
4 Roll out dough, ¼ at a time, ⅛ inch thick, on a lightly floured pastry cloth or board. Cut out with a floured small "gingerbread man" cutter or cut around your own cardboard pattern; place, 1 inch apart, on greased cookie sheets. Reroll and cut out all trimmings. Decorate with cut-up currants for eyes, mouth, and buttons.
5 Bake in moderate oven (350°) 6 minutes, or until firm. Remove from cookie sheets; cool completely on wire racks. Store in a tightly covered container.

594

Merry Cut-Outs
Here's baking magic: Cut the same design in the center of each two cookies, then switch the centers.
Bake at 350° for 10 minutes. Makes about 7 dozen medium-size cookies

3½ cups sifted all-purpose flour
1 teaspoon baking powder
½ teaspoon salt
1 cup (2 sticks) butter or margarine
1½ cups sugar
2 eggs
1½ teaspoons vanilla

¼ teaspoon lemon extract
  Yellow, green, and red food colorings
¼ teaspoon almond extract
  Few drops peppermint extract
¼ teaspoon orange extract

1 Measure flour, baking powder, and salt into sifter.
2 Cream butter or margarine with sugar until fluffy-light in a large bowl; beat in eggs and vanilla.
3 Sift in flour mixture, a third at a time, blending well to make a stiff dough. Divide into quarters and place in separate bowls.
4 Stir lemon extract and a few drops yellow food coloring into dough in one bowl; stir almond extract and a few drops green food coloring into second bowl; stir peppermint extract and a few drops red food coloring into third bowl; stir orange extract into fourth.
5 Wrap each dough in wax paper or transparent wrap; chill several hours, or until firm enough to roll. (Overnight is best.)
6 Roll out half each of the yellow and green doughs, ⅛ inch thick, on a lightly floured pastry cloth or board; cut out each with a 2½-inch round or fluted cutter, then cut a fancy shape from center of each with a truffle cutter.
7 Place large cookies, 1 inch apart, on ungreased cookie sheets. Fit small yellow cutouts in centers of green cookies and small green cut-outs in centers of yellow cookies. Repeat with remaining doughs.
8 Bake in moderate oven (350°) 10 minutes, or until firm. Remove from cookie sheets; cool on wire racks. Store in a tightly covered container.

Lemon Leaves
"Frosting" of pistachio nuts, lemon rind, and sugar bakes right on these tiny delicacies.
Bake at 350° for 6 to 7 minutes. Makes about 25 dozen tiny cookies

2¼ cups sifted all-purpose flour
3 teaspoons baking powder
½ teaspoon salt
½ cup (1 stick) butter or margarine
1⅓ cups sugar
1 egg
1 tablespoon light cream or table cream
1 teaspoon lemon extract
2 egg yolks
1 teaspoon water
¼ cup finely chopped pistachio nuts
1½ teaspoons grated lemon rind

1 Measure flour, baking powder, and salt into sifter.

Snowy white and pastel pink Meringue Miniatures, thin Lemon Leaves, and marquis-cut Crown Jewels.

2 Cream butter or margarine and 1 cup sugar until fluffy in large bowl. (Save remaining ⅓ cup sugar for Step 5.) Beat in egg, cream, and lemon extract.

3 Sift in dry ingredients, a third at a time, blending well to make a soft dough. Chill several hours (overnight is best), or until firm enough to roll easily.

4 Roll out, a quarter at a time, very thin (1/16 inch), on a lightly floured pastry cloth or board. Cut into leaf or other fancy shape with a floured tiny cookie or truffle cutter. Place on greased cookie sheets.

5 Mix egg yolks with water in a cup; strain. Mix saved ⅓ cup sugar, pistachio nuts, and grated lemon rind in second cup. Brush cookies with egg-yolk mixture, then sprinkle with nut-lemon mixture.

6 Bake in moderate oven (350°) 6 to 7 minutes, or until firm but not brown. Remove carefully from cookie sheets; cool on wire racks. To store stack only a few layers. They're fragile!

Crown Jewels

Bright jelly filling twinkles atop each of these buttery gems.
Bake at 400° for 8 minutes. Makes 5 dozen

1½ cups sifted all-purpose flour
1½ teaspoons baking powder
 ½ teaspoon salt
  4 tablespoons (½ stick) butter or margarine
 ¾ cup sugar
  1 egg, separated
 ¼ teaspoon vanilla or brandy flavoring
  2 tablespoons milk
 ¼ cup each mint, peach, and red-currant jelly
     Silver candies

596

1 Measure flour, baking powder, and salt into sifter.

2 Cream butter or margarine and ½ cup sugar until fluffy in medium-size bowl; beat in egg yolk and vanilla or brandy flavoring. (Save remaining ¼ cup sugar and egg white for topping in Step 6.)

3 Sift in dry ingredients, a third at a time, adding alternately with milk; stir just until well-blended. Chill for several hours, or until firm enough to roll easily.

4 Roll out, a quarter at a time, to a ⅛-inch thickness on lightly floured pastry cloth or board. Cut into ovals or rounds with a floured

2-inch cutter, then cut a small oval or circle in middle of half the cookies and lift out with tip of knife. (Save to reroll and cut out along with trimmings.)

5 Place whole ovals or rounds on greased cookie sheets; spoon about ½ teaspoonful of mint, peach, or red-currant jelly in middle of each. Top, sandwich style, with a cutout oval or round; press edges together lightly with a fork or thumb to seal. Reroll trimmings, cut out, and fill.

6 Beat saved egg white slightly in a cup; brush over cookies. Sprinkle lightly with saved ¼ cup sugar; decorate with silver candies.

7 Bake in hot oven (400°) 8 minutes, or until golden. Cool on cookie sheets about 5 minutes, then remove carefully. Cool on wire racks. Stack not more than two layers high, with wax paper or transparent wrap between, on tray or in open pan.

Chocolate Mushrooms

A round cutter and your fingers speed shaping. Recipe makes lots, but dough keeps well in the refrigerator to bake as you please.
Bake at 350° for 8 minutes. Makes about 20 dozen tiny cookies

2¼ cups sifted all-purpose flour
1½ teaspoons baking powder
 ½ teaspoon baking soda
 ¼ teaspoon salt
 ½ cup (1 stick) butter or margarine
  1 cup granulated sugar
  2 eggs
  3 squares unsweetened chocolate, melted and cooled
 ½ teaspoon vanilla
  5 drops red food coloring
2½ cups 10X (confectioners' powdered) sugar
  5 tablespoons water
  1 square semisweet chocolate, coarsely grated

1 Measure flour, baking powder, soda, and salt into sifter.

2 Cream butter or margarine with granulated sugar until fluffy in a large bowl; beat in eggs, melted chocolate, vanilla, and food coloring.

3 Sift in flour mixture, a third at a time, blending well to make a stiff dough. Wrap in wax paper or transparent wrap; chill several hours, or until firm enough to roll. (Overnight is best.)

4 Roll out dough, ⅛ at a time, ⅛ inch thick on a lightly floured pastry cloth or board. Cut out 1½-inch rounds with a floured cutter; lift away all trimmings. Then, with same cutter, cut an oval-shape piece from each round, leaving a section shaped like a mushroom cap.

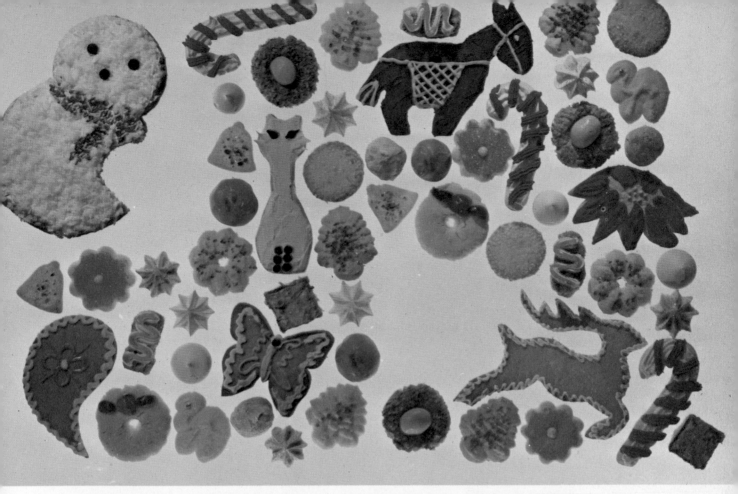

All dressed up for the holiday season, a collection of cut-outs, spritz, shaped, drop and bar cookies.

5 Place oval cut-outs, 2 inches apart, on greased cookie sheets; shape each with fingers into a "mushroom stem." Lift caps and place, slightly overlapping, on stems; press gently to hold in place. Reroll and cut out all trimmings.

6 Bake in moderate oven (350°) 8 minutes, or just until firm. Remove from cookie sheets; cool completely on wire racks. Store in a tightly covered container until ready to frost.

7 Blend 10X sugar and water until smooth in a small bowl; drizzle over cookies; sprinkle with grated chocolate. Let stand on wire racks until frosting is firm.

Pinwheels

So rich they literally melt in your mouth! Whipped cream goes into the unusual pastrylike dough.

Bake at 350° for 15 minutes. Makes about 5 dozen tiny cookies

1 cup sifted all-purpose flour
½ teaspoon baking powder
6 tablespoons (¾ stick) butter or margarine
½ cup cream for whipping
⅔ cup strawberry jam (not preserves)

1 Sift flour and baking powder into a large bowl; cut in butter or margarine until mixture is crumbly.

2 Beat cream until stiff in a small bowl; stir into flour mixture, blending well to make a stiff dough. Wrap in wax paper or transparent wrap; chill several hours, or until firm enough to roll. (Overnight is best.)

3 Roll out dough, ¼ at a time, to an 8-inch square on a lightly floured pastry cloth or board; cut into 16 two-inch squares. Starting at each corner, cut diagonally through dough 1 inch in toward center.

4 Spoon a rounded ¼ teaspoonful jam in center of each square; moisten corners with water, then pick up every other corner point and fold to center, overlapping slightly; press lightly to seal. Place, 1 inch apart, on greased cookie sheets.

5 Bake in moderate oven (350°) 15 minutes,

597

More of FAMILY CIRCLE's favorite holiday cookies tumbling out of their cannister cornucopia, lovingly baked and artfully decorated. Recipes are included throughout this section, also tips for frosting.

or until firm and lightly golden. Remove from cookie sheets; cool completely on wire racks. Store in a tightly covered container.

Taffy Twinkle Stars

They're like crispy shortbread with the rich flavor of old-fashioned molasses.
Bake at 325° for 15 minutes. Makes about 8 dozen

    1 cup (2 sticks) butter or margarine
    ½ cup molasses
    2 teaspoons vanilla
    2 cups sifted all-purpose flour
    1 cup unsifted 10X (confectioners' powdered)
      sugar
    1 tablespoon water
      Silver candies

1 Blend butter or margarine with molasses in medium-size bowl; stir in 1 teaspoon vanilla. (Save remaining teaspoon for frosting in Step 4.) Gradually blend in flour. Chill overnight.
2 Roll out, a small amount at a time, to ¼-inch thickness on lightly floured pastry cloth or board. Cut out with floured star-shape cutters of varying sizes, or cut around your own cardboard patterns with a sharp knife. Place on ungreased cookie sheets.
3 Bake in slow oven (325°) 15 minutes, or until firm. Remove from cookie sheets; cool completely on wire racks.
4 Blend 10X sugar, water, and saved 1 teaspoon of vanilla until smooth in small bowl. Frost cookies; decorate centers with silver candies.

Holly Wreaths

Berries and leaves of colored frostings trim butter cookies.
Bake at 350° for 10 minutes. Makes about 4 dozen

    1 cup (2 sticks) butter or margarine
    1 cup granulated sugar
    3 egg yolks
    1½ teaspoons vanilla
    2½ cups sifted all-purpose flour
      Green decorating sugar
      Red and green decorating frostings in pressurized cans or plastic tubes

1 Cream butter or margarine with granulated sugar until fluffy-light in a large bowl; beat in egg yolks and vanilla.
2 Stir in flour, a third at a time, blending well to make a stiff dough. Wrap in wax paper or transparent wrap and chill several hours, or until firm enough to roll. (Overnight is best.)

3 Roll out dough, one quarter at a time, ¼ inch thick on a lightly floured pastry cloth or board. Cut into circles with a lightly floured doughnut cutter. Or cut into rounds with a 2½-inch fluted cutter, then cut a 1-inch round from center of each. Place circles, ½ inch apart, on ungreased cookie sheets; sprinkle lightly with green decorating sugar. Reroll all trimmings and cut out.
4 Bake in moderate oven (350°) 10 minutes, or until firm. Remove carefully from cookie sheets to wire racks; cool completely. Decorate with holly berries and leaves, using frostings in pressurized cans or plastic tubes.

Pepparkakor

Bake at 350° for 7 minutes. Makes about 8 dozen

    1⅔ cups sifted all-purpose flour
    ½ teaspoon baking soda
    ½ teaspoon salt
    ¾ teaspoon ground ginger
    ½ teaspoon ground cinnamon
    ¼ teaspoon ground cloves
    ¼ teaspoon ground cardamom
    6 tablespoons (¾ stick) butter or margarine
    ⅓ cup sugar
    ¼ cup light molasses
    1 teaspoon grated orange rind
    ¼ cup finely chopped toasted almonds
      ORNAMENTAL FROSTING (see index for recipe
      page number)

1 Sift flour, soda, salt, ginger, cinnamon, cloves, and cardamom on wax paper.
2 Cream butter or margarine with sugar until fluffy-light in a large bowl; beat in molasses, orange rind, and almonds. Stir in flour mixture, a third at a time, blending well to make a stiff dough. Chill several hours, or overnight, until firm enough to roll.
3 Roll out dough, one third at a time, ⅛ inch thick, on a lightly floured pastry cloth or board; cut into fancy shapes with floured 2-inch cookie cutters. Place, 1 inch apart, on lightly greased large cookie sheets. Reroll and cut out all trimmings.
4 Bake in moderate oven (350°) 7 minutes, or until firm. Remove from cookie sheets to wire racks; cool completely.
5 Make ORNAMENTAL FROSTING. Fit a writing tip onto a cake-decorating set; fill with frosting. Press out onto cookies in designs of your choice; let stand until frosting is firm.

Scandinavian Cut-Outs

Fancy-shaped and frosted, these hang on Christmas trees in their native lands.

599

COOKIE JAR JEWELS

ORANGE BELL

FANTASY FLOWER

FANTASY PONY

Bake at 350° for 7 minutes. Makes about 2 dozen

      3 cups sifted all-purpose flour
 1½ teaspoons baking powder
      1 teaspoon salt
   ¼ teaspoon ground ginger
   ¼ teaspoon ground nutmeg
   ¾ cup honey
   ⅓ cup firmly packed brown sugar
   ⅓ cup butter or margarine
   ¼ cup very finely chopped candied citron
         (from a 4-ounce jar)
      1 teaspoon grated lemon rind
         Colored decorating frostings in pressurized
         cans or plastic tubes

1 Measure flour, baking powder, salt, ginger, and nutmeg into a sifter.
2 Heat honey and brown sugar to boiling in a small saucepan. Pour over butter or margarine in a large bowl; stir until butter melts; cool to lukewarm. Stir in citron and lemon rind.
3 Sift in flour mixture, a third at a time, blending well to make a stiff dough. Turn out onto a lightly floured pastry cloth or board; knead 2 to 3 minutes. Wrap in wax paper or transparent wrap; chill several hours, or until firm enough to roll. (Overnight is best.)
4 Roll out dough, half at a time, ⅛ inch thick on a lightly floured pastry cloth or board. Cut into fancy shapes with floured 4-inch cutters, or cut around your own cardboard patterns. Place cut-outs, 1 inch apart, on greased cookie sheets. Reroll all trimmings and cut out.
5 Bake in moderate oven (350°) 7 minutes, or until firm. Remove from cookie sheets to wire racks; cool completely. Store, loosely covered,

at least one week to mellow and soften, then decorate with designs of your choice, using frostings in pressurized cans or plastic tubes.

●

Cut-Out Fantasies
Bake at 350° for 8 minutes. Makes about 4 dozen 4-inch cutouts

   4 cups sifted all-purpose flour
   4 teaspoons baking powder
   ½ teaspoon salt
   ⅓ cup butter or margarine
   ⅓ cup firmly packed light brown sugar
   ⅔ cup light molasses
   1 egg
   1 teaspoon vanilla
      ORNAMENTAL FROSTING (see index for recipe
         page number)
   1 envelope (1 ounce) liquid unsweetened
      chocolate
      Yellow, red, and green food colorings

1 Sift flour, baking powder, and salt onto wax paper.
2 Cream butter or margarine with brown sugar until fluffy-light in a medium-size bowl; beat in molasses, egg, and vanilla.
3 Stir in flour mixture, a third at a time, blending well to make a stiff dough. Chill several hours, or overnight, until firm enough to roll.
4 Roll out dough, one quarter at a time, ⅛ inch thick, on a lightly floured pastry cloth or board;

cut into animal, flower, ornament, or other fancy shapes with a floured cookie cutter, or cut around your own cardboard patterns with a sharp knife. Place, 1 inch apart, on greased large cookie sheets.

5 Bake in moderate oven (350°) 8 minutes, or until firm but not brown. Remove from cookie sheets to wire racks; cool completely.

6 Make ORNAMENTAL FROSTING. Stir in chocolate, or tint yellow, pink, or green with food colorings; frost and decorate cookies, following pictured ideas.

Gingerbread Dancing Dolls

To hang on the tree . . . to wrap for giving.
Bake at 350° for 10 minutes. Makes 6 ten-inch cookies

  3 cups sifted all-purpose flour
  3 teaspoons baking powder
1½ teaspoons ground ginger
  ½ teaspoon salt
  ⅓ cup butter, margarine, or vegetable shortening
  ⅓ cup firmly packed brown sugar
  ⅔ cup molasses
  1 egg, unbeaten
    CREAMY FROSTING (see index for recipe)
    Packaged gumdrops
    Red Cinnamon Candies
    Tinted coconut
    Silver candies

1 Measure flour, baking powder, ginger, and salt into sifter.

2 Cream shortening until soft in medium-size bowl; gradually add brown sugar, creaming after each addition until mixture is light and fluffy; beat in molasses and egg.

3 Sift in dry ingredients; blend well (dough will be stiff); cover; chill about 2 hours, or until firm enough to roll.

4 While dough chills, draw and cut out a 10-inch-tall doll pattern from lightweight cardboard.

5 Divide chilled dough into sixths; roll out, one at a time, to a rectangle, 8x10, on a lightly greased cookie sheet; lay pattern on top and cut around with tip of sharp-pointed knife; remove excess dough.

6 Bake 1 or 2 cookies at a time in moderate oven (350°) 10 minutes, or until firm on top.

7 Remove from cookie sheet with spatula; cool on wire cake rack.

8 Decorate with green-tinted CREAMY FROSTING (see index for recipe page number), spread thickly in design for dress; draw on shoes, face, hair, and bracelet with wooden pick dipped in white or tinted frosting. While still moist, decorate dress with thinly sliced gumdrops; face with cinnamon candies for eyes and mouth; hair with tinted coconut; bracelet with silver candies; dry thoroughly.

Orange Bells

Bake at 350° about 6 minutes. Makes about 25 dozen tiny cookies

2¼ cups sifted all-purpose flour
  3 teaspoons baking powder
  ½ teaspoon salt
  ½ cup (1 stick) butter or margarine
1⅓ cups sugar
  1 whole egg
  1 tablespoon cream
1½ teaspoons orange extract
  2 egg yolks
  1 teaspoon water
  ¼ cup finely chopped pistachio nuts
1½ teaspoons grated orange rind

1 Sift flour, baking powder, and salt onto wax paper.

2 Cream butter or margarine and 1 cup of the sugar until fluffy-light in a large bowl. Beat in whole egg, cream, and orange extract.

3 Stir in flour mixture, a third at a time, blending well to make a soft dough. Chill several hours, or overnight, until firm enough to roll.

4 Roll out, a quarter at a time, 1/16 inch thick, on a lightly floured pastry cloth or board. Cut into bell shapes with a floured tiny cookie cutter. Place on greased large cookie sheets.

5 Mix egg yolks with water in a cup; strain. Mix remaining ⅓ cup sugar, pistachio nuts, and grated orange rind in a second cup. Brush cookies with egg-yolk mixture, then sprinkle with orange mixture.

6 Bake in moderate oven (350°) 6 to 7 minutes, or until firm but not brown. Remove carefully from cookie sheets to wire racks; cool completely.

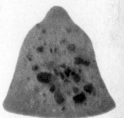

Cardamom Stars

Bake at 375° for 7 minutes. Makes about 13 dozen

2¾ cups sifted all-purpose flour
  ¾ teaspoon baking powder
  ½ teaspoon baking soda
  ½ teaspoon salt
  ½ teaspoon ground cardamom
  ½ cup (1 stick) butter or margarine
  ¾ cup firmly packed light brown sugar
  1 egg
  ½ teaspoon vanilla
  ¼ cup dairy sour cream

601

PINK GLAZE *(recipe follows)*
ORNAMENTAL FROSTING *(See index for recipe page number)*

1 Sift flour, baking powder, soda, salt, and cardamom onto wax paper.
2 Cream butter or margarine with brown sugar until fluffy-light in a large bowl; beat in egg and vanilla. Stir in flour mixture, a third at a time, alternately with sour cream, blending well to make a stiff dough. Chill several hours, or overnight, until firm enough to roll.
3 Roll out dough, one quarter at a time, ⅛ inch thick, on a lightly floured pastry cloth or board; cut into star shapes with a floured 1½-inch cookie cutter. Place, 1 inch apart, on lightly greased large cookie sheets. Reroll and cut out all trimmings.
4 Bake in moderate oven (375°) 7 minutes, or until firm and lightly browned. Remove from cookie sheets to wire racks; cool completely.
5 Make PINK GLAZE. Place cookies in a single layer on wire racks set over wax paper; spoon glaze over each to cover completely. (Scrape glaze that drips onto paper back into bowl and beat until smooth before using again.) Let cookies stand until glaze is firm.
6 Make ORNAMENTAL FROSTING. Fit a writing tip onto a cake-decorating set; fill with frosting. Press out onto cookies to resemble rays of stars.

PINK GLAZE—Sift 1 package (1 pound) 10X (confectioners' powdered) sugar into a medium-size bowl; beat in 6 tablespoons water until mixture is smooth. Tint pink with a few drops red food coloring. (If frosting stiffens as you work, beat in a little more water, a drop or two at a time, until thin enough to pour from a spoon.)

602

Shortbread Sparkler Buds
Tops twinkle invitingly with a sunny baked-on sugar "frosting."
Bake at 325° for 18 to 20 minutes. Makes 5 dozen

1 cup (2 sticks) butter or margarine
½ cup very fine granulated sugar
2 cups sifted all-purpose flour
  Yellow decorating sugar

1 Cream butter or margarine with sugar until fluffy in a medium-size bowl; blend in flour gradually, then beat at medium speed with an electric beater 5 minutes, or knead with hands until satin-smooth.
2 Pat out to a rectangle, 9x6, on an ungreased cookie sheet; chill several hours, or until firm enough to hold its shape when cut. (Overnight is even better.)
3 Cut into rounds with a floured 1-inch cutter; place on ungreased cookie sheets. Sprinkle generously with decorating sugar; chill 30 minutes before baking. Pat out trimmings ¾ inch thick, chill, and cut, following Steps 2 and 3.
4 Bake in slow oven (325°) 18 to 20 minutes, or until firm in centers and lightly golden around edges. Remove from cookie sheets; cool completely on wire racks.

Sugar Sparklers
They're buttery old-fashioned sugar cookies with a speedy up-to-date rolling trick.
Bake at 350° for 10 minutes. Makes about 6 dozen

3 cups sifted all-purpose flour
1 teaspoon baking powder
½ teaspoon salt
¾ cup (1½ sticks) butter or margarine
1 cup sugar
2 eggs
1 teaspoon vanilla

1 Measure flour, baking powder, and salt into sifter.
2 Cream butter or margarine with sugar until fluffy in large bowl; beat in 1 egg. Separate remaining egg and beat in yolk, then vanilla. (Save white.)
3 Sift in dry ingredients, a quarter at a time, blending well to make a stiff dough. Chill 1 hour, or until firm enough to roll.
4 Divide dough into quarters; roll, one at a time, to ⅛-inch thickness on greased cookie sheet. (Set cookie sheet on damp towel to keep it from slipping.) Cut into diamonds with pastry wheel or sharp knife. Brush with saved egg white, slightly beaten; sprinkle with sugar, if you wish.
5 Bake in moderate oven (350°) 10 minutes, or until firm. Separate and remove from cookie sheets with long spatula; cool on wire racks.

Spicy Crisps
Typically Danish, they are wafer-thin and rich with citron and almonds.
Bake at 375° for 8 to 10 minutes. Makes about 8 dozen

2¼ cups sifted all-purpose flour
¼ teaspoon baking soda
1 teaspoon cinnamon

Shortbread cut into chunky stars and brightened with yellow sugar, Sesame Wafers and crispy Sugar Cookies.

COOKIE JAR JEWELS

½ teaspoon ground cloves
½ cup dark corn syrup
¼ cup sugar
4 tablespoons (½ stick) butter or margarine
¼ cup finely chopped almonds
2 tablespoons finely chopped candied citron
½ teaspoon grated lemon rind

1 Sift flour, soda, cinnamon, and cloves into a small bowl.
2 Combine syrup, sugar, and butter or margarine in a medium-size saucepan; heat, stirring constantly, just to boiling. Pour into a medium-size bowl; stir in almonds, citron, and lemon rind.
3 Stir in flour mixture, half at a time, blending well to make a stiff dough. Cover bowl and let stand at room temperature for 2 days to ripen.
4 When ready to roll dough, knead until smooth on a lightly floured pastry cloth or board. Roll out, half at a time, 1/16 inch thick; cut into rounds with a floured 2-inch plain or fluted cutter. Place, not touching, on greased cookie sheets. Brush very lightly with water; top each with a piece of candied cherry or fruit peel, if you wish. Repeat with remaining dough, then reroll and cut out all trimmings.
5 Bake in moderate oven (375°) 8 to 10 minutes, or until firm and brown. Remove from cookie sheets; cool completely on wire racks. (If you wish to bake only half of the cookies at one time, wrap remaining dough and keep chilled. Before rolling, knead again.)

Medallions
One batch of dough makes enough for the base cookies, plus the fancy colored toppers.
Bake at 375° for 10 to 15 minutes. Makes 5 dozen double cookies

4¼ cups sifted all-purpose flour
¼ teaspoon salt
1½ cups (3 sticks) butter or margarine
1 cup sugar
1 egg
1 teaspoon vanilla
½ teaspoon almond extract
   Red and green food colorings
   ALMOND FROSTING (recipe follows)

1 Sift 4 cups of the flour and salt into a medium-size bowl. Set remaining ¼ cup flour aside for Step 3.
2 Cream butter or margarine with sugar until fluffy in a large bowl; beat in egg and vanilla. Stir in flour mixture, a third at a time, blending well to make a soft dough.
3 Divide dough in half; stir remaining ¼ cup flour into one half for making rounds for base;

set aside for Step 5. Divide remaining half in two equal parts; place each in a small bowl.
4 Blend ¼ teaspoon of the almond extract and enough red food coloring into dough in one bowl to tint a delicate pink, and remaining ¼ teaspoon almond extract and enough green food coloring into dough in second bowl to tint light green. Chill tinted doughs 30 minutes, or until slightly firm.
5 Roll out plain dough, ⅛ inch thick, on a lightly floured pastry cloth or board; cut into rounds with a floured 2½-inch plain or fluted cutter. Place, 1 inch apart, on ungreased cookie sheets.
6 Fit star plate or disk on cookie press; fill with pink dough; press out onto ungreased cookie sheets. Fit press with sunburst plate or disk; repeat with green dough.
7 Bake all in moderate oven (375°) 10 minutes for plain cookies, and 15 minutes for tinted ones, or until firm. Remove from cookie sheets; cool completely on wire racks.
8 Place about ¼ teaspoonful ALMOND FROSTING in the center of each plain cookie; top with a tinted one. Let stand until frosting sets.

ALMOND FROSTING—Mix ¾ cup 10X (confectioners' powdered) sugar with 2 teaspoons water, 1 teaspoon vanilla, and ¼ teaspoon almond extract until smooth in a small bowl. Makes about ½ cup.

Jolly Snowmen
Bake at 350° for 10 minutes. Makes 2 dozen

3¼ cups sifted all-purpose flour
1 teaspoon baking powder
½ teaspoon salt
1 cup (2 sticks) butter or margarine
1 cup sugar
2 eggs
1 teaspoon lemon extract
1 package creamy white frosting mix
1 package (7 ounces) cookie coconut
   Green and red decorating sprinkles
   Tiny chocolate decorating rounds

1 Sift flour, baking powder, and salt onto wax paper.
2 Cream ¾ cup (1½ sticks) of the butter or margarine with sugar until fluffy-light in a large bowl; beat in eggs and lemon extract. Stir in flour mixture, a third at a time, blending well to make a stiff dough. Chill several hours, or overnight, until firm enough to roll.
3 Roll out dough, one quarter at a time, ⅛ inch thick, on a lightly floured pastry cloth or board; cut into snowman shapes with a large floured cutter, or cut around your own cardboard pattern with a sharp knife. Place, 1 inch apart, on

JOLLY SNOWMAN

PEPPARKAKOR DEER

ROBIN'S NEST

large cookie sheets. Reroll and cut out all trimmings.

4 Bake in moderate oven (350°) 10 minutes, or until firm and lightly golden. Remove from cookie sheets to wire racks; cool completely.

5 Prepare frosting mix with remaining ¼ cup butter or margarine and water, following label directions; spread a heaping tablespoonful on each cooky; sprinkle generously with coconut. Press green and red sprinkles into frosting to resemble a scarf, and set chocolate rounds in place for eyes and nose. Let cookies stand until frosting is firm.

●

Brown Sugar Shortbread Stars
Buttery-rich, and worth every calorie.
Bake at 275° for 30 minutes. Makes about 2 dozen cookies

1 cup (½ pound) butter or margarine*
½ cup sifted brown sugar, firmly packed
2 cups sifted all-purpose flour
  Multicolor sprinkles
  Silver candies

1 Cream butter or margarine until soft in medium-size bowl; gradually add brown sugar, creaming after each addition until mixture is light and fluffy.

2 Sift in flour gradually, blending well; knead on lightly floured pastry cloth or board 10 to 15 minutes, or until smooth and firm, adding only enough additional flour to keep dough from sticking.

3 Roll out to ½-inch thickness; cut with floured star-shape cookie cutter; transfer to ungreased cookie sheets with wide spatula or pancake turner; decorate star points with sprinkles and candies.

4 Bake in very slow oven (275°) 30 minutes, or until lightly browned around edges.

5 Remove from cookie sheets with spatula; cool on wire cake racks.

*Or use part vegetable shortening.

605

WHO'S WHO OF COOKIES

1. Scandinavian Cut-Outs. 2. Viennese Rounds. 3. Cherry Macaroon Puffs. 4. Sesame Lace Wafers. 5. Sugar Cookies cut into wreaths. 6. Almond Cooky Cuplets. 7. Meringue tinted green and shaped into trees.

Anise Shortbread Roses
Bake at 325° for 20 minutes. Makes about 5 dozen cookies

1 cup (2 sticks) butter or margarine
½ cup very fine granulated sugar
¼ teaspoon anise extract
2¼ cups sifted all-purpose flour
Pink decorating sugar
Tiny yellow candies

1 Cream butter or margarine with granulated sugar until fluffy-light in a large bowl; beat in anise extract.
2 Stir in flour, one third at a time, blending well to make a stiff dough. Knead 10 to 15 minutes, or until smooth. Chill several hours, or overnight, until firm enough to handle.
3 Roll or pat out dough, one quarter at a time, ¼ inch thick, on a lightly floured pastry cloth or board. Cut into small rounds with a 1½-inch scalloped cutter. Place, 1 inch apart, on large cookie sheets. Reroll and cut out all trimmings.
4 Sprinkle cookies with pink sugar; place a yellow candy in center of each.
5 Bake in slow oven (325°) 20 minutes, or until firm but not brown. Remove from cookie sheets to wire racks; cool completely.

●

"Paintbox" Christmas Cookies
Bake at 350° for 10 minutes. Makes 8 cookies

4 cups sifted all-purpose flour
2 teaspoons baking powder
1 teaspoon salt
¾ cups (1½ sticks) butter or margarine
1½ cups sugar
2 eggs
2 teaspoons vanilla
1 teaspoon lemon extract
Cookie "Paint"
5 egg yolks
2 teaspoons water
Food coloring

1 Sift the all-purpose flour, baking powder and salt onto wax paper.
2 Beat butter or margarine with sugar until fluffy light in a large bowl. Beat in eggs, vanilla and lemon extract. Stir in flour mixture, a third at a time, to make a stiff dough.
3 Beat egg yolks for "paint" with water in large bowl.
4 Divide egg-yolk mixture equally into five fruit-juice glasses. Add drops of different food coloring into each of four glasses. (The more you add, the deeper the color will be.) To make dark outline "paint," add blue, green and red food coloring into fifth glass.

5 Roll out a portion of cookie dough to a rectangle ¼" thick on wax paper. Moisten tabletop to prevent slipping.
6 Cut out pictures shown on these pages for patterns. Place patterns on dough. Cut out shapes with sharp-pointed utility knife and trim away excess.
7 Punch holes through the pattern with a hat pin or needle along all the inside lines of figure details.
8 Lift off pattern.
9 With small artist's brush, apply dark outline "paint" to punched design.
10 Fill in all solid-colored areas as indicated on the patterns. Be sure to spread the paint thickly to prevent it from cracking during baking.
11 With a broad pancake turner, transfer cookies to lightly greased cookie sheets.
12 Repeat with remaining dough.
13 Bake in moderate oven (375°) for 10 minutes, or until firm and lightly golden in unpainted areas. Remove from cookie sheets to wire racks; cool completely.
Note: If you wish to hang the cookies on the tree, thread a needle with 8" of thread and run it through the cookie, at least 2" from the top. Tie ends to make hanger for attaching to tree. Shorter thread can be used if you wish to use a metal tree hanger.

607

The newest way to decorate cookies is to "paint" them.

HOW TO MAKE "PAINTBOX" CHRISTMAS COOKIES

Roll out the dough to a thickness of ¼" between two sheets of wax paper.

With a small paintbrush, apply dark outline "paint" to the punched design.

Using the pictures on p.p. 607 and 609 as a pattern, cut out with a sharp knife.

Fill in solid areas with appropriate "paint" to follow the pictures shown.

608

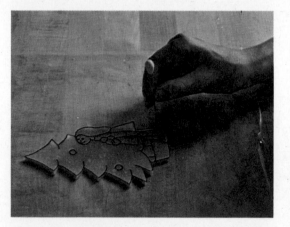

Punch holes through the pattern with a hatpin to outline the figure details.

Be sure to apply the "paint" thickly in order to prevent it from cracking.

CUT OUT PICTURES FOR PATTERNS

609

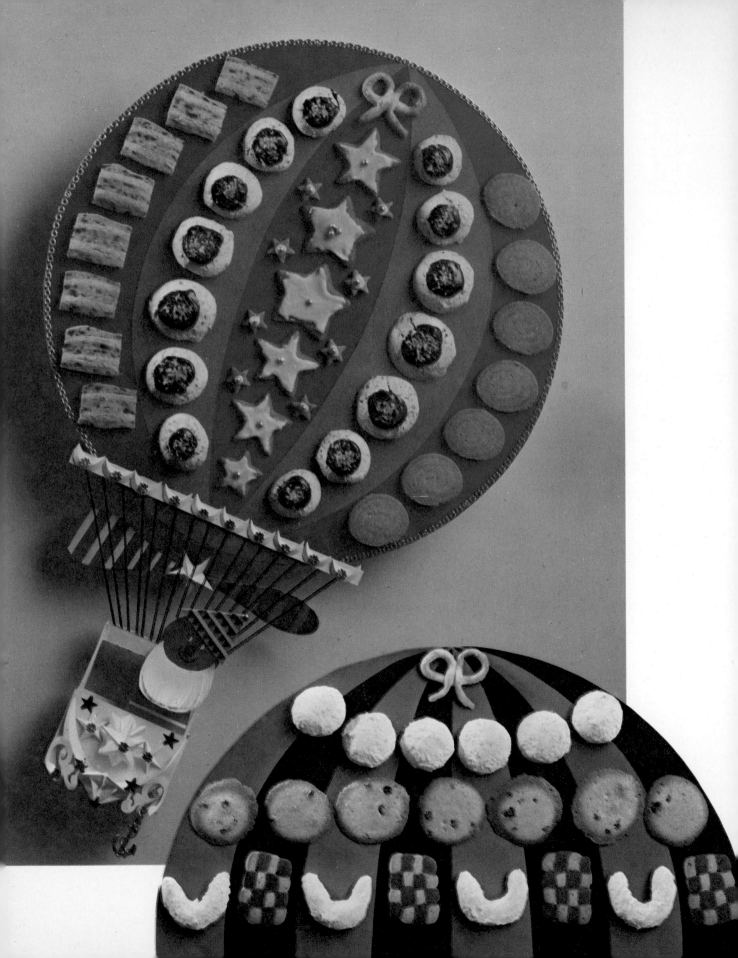

REFRIGERATOR COOKIES

Slice-a-Fancy Cookies

Bake at 350° for 10 minutes. Makes about 12 dozen

    4 cups sifted all-purpose flour
    1 teaspoon baking powder
    1 teaspoon salt
    ¼ teaspoon baking soda
    1¼ cups (2½ sticks) butter or margarine
    1 cup firmly packed light brown sugar
    ½ cup granulated sugar
    2 eggs
    2 teaspoons vanilla

1 Sift flour, baking powder, salt, and baking soda onto wax paper.
2 Beat butter or margarine with brown and granulated sugars until fluffy-light in a large bowl; beat in eggs and vanilla. Stir in flour mixture, a third at a time, blending well to make a soft dough.
3 Divide evenly into 3 bowls. Flavor, shape, and decorate each variety, following recipes below.
4 Bake all cookies in moderate oven (350°) 10 minutes, or until golden. Remove from cookie sheets to wire racks; cool completely.

Ribbon Fancies

Divide one bowl of dough in half. Tint one half green with a few drops of green food coloring; leave other half plain. Roll out each half to a 9x3-inch rectangle between sheets of wax paper; chill in freezer 10 minutes; halve each rectangle lengthwise, cutting through wax paper; peel off top sheets. Brush tops very lightly with milk. Lay one plain strip, paper side up, on top of green strip and peel off paper; repeat with remaining strips, alternating colors, to make 4 layers. Wrap in wax paper or foil; chill several hours, or freeze, until very firm. When ready to bake, unwrap dough and slice into ⅛ inch-thick rectangles with a sharp knife; place on greased large cookie sheets. Bake and cool, following directions for SLICE-A-FANCY COOKIES.

Pinwheel Twirls

Divide second bowl of dough in half. Tint one half deep pink with a few drops of red food coloring; leave other half plain. Roll out each half to a 9x9-inch square between sheets of wax

Ribbon Fancies (far left), Pinwheel Twirls (far right) and Checkerboards (below) are three favorite, fancy ways to shape refrigerator cookies. They're not hard.

paper; peel off top sheets. Lay pink-tinted dough, paper side up, on top of plain dough; peel off paper. Roll up doughs tightly, jelly-roll fashion. Wrap in wax paper or foil; chill until very firm. When ready to bake, unwrap dough and slice into ⅛ inch-thick rounds with a sharp knife; place on greased large cookie sheets. Bake and cool, following directions for SLICE-A-FANCY COOKIES.

Checkerboards

Divide third bowl of dough in half. Blend ½ square unsweetened chocolate, melted and cooled, into one half; leave other half plain. Roll out each half to a 9x3-inch rectangle between sheets of wax paper; chill. Peel off top sheets. Cut each rectangle lengthwise into 8 strips, each ⅜ inch wide. Carefully lift a chocolate strip with a long-blade spatula and place on a clean sheet of wax paper or foil; lay a plain strip close to it, then repeat with a chocolate and plain strip to make a four-stripe ribbon, about 1½ inches wide. Brush very lightly with milk. Build a second, third, and fourth layer, alternating plain and chocolate strips each time and brushing each layer with milk before adding the next one. Wrap in wax paper or foil; chill. When ready to bake, unwrap dough and slice ⅛ inch-thick rectangles with a sharp knife; place on greased large cookie sheets. Bake and cool, following directions for SLICE-A-FANCY COOKIES.

Strawberry Jim-Jams

Jam-and-walnut filling twirls inside these buttery pinwheels.
Bake at 375° for 10 minutes. Makes 4 dozen

    2 cups sifted all-purpose flour
    ½ teaspoon baking powder
    ½ teaspoon ground nutmeg
    ¼ teaspoon salt
    ½ cup (1 stick) butter or margarine
    ½ cup granulated sugar
    ¼ cup firmly packed brown sugar
    1 egg
    1 teaspoon vanilla
    ½ cup finely chopped walnuts (from a 4-ounce can)
    ½ cup strawberry jam (from a 12-ounce jar)

1 Sift regular flour, baking powder, nutmeg, and salt into a small bowl.
2 Cream butter or margarine with granulated and brown sugars until fluffy in a large bowl; beat in egg and vanilla.

611

3 Stir in flour mixture, half at a time, blending well to make a stiff dough. Chill dough several hours, or until it is firm enough to roll. (Overnight is even better.)
4 Roll out dough to a rectangle, 15x12, on a lightly floured pastry cloth or board. Mix walnuts and jam in a small bowl; spread evenly over dough; roll up, jelly-roll fashion. (Be sure walnuts are chopped fine, or cookies will crack when rolled.) Wrap in wax paper or transparent wrap. Chill overnight, or until very firm.
5 When ready to bake, unwrap dough and slice into ¼-inch-thick rounds with a sharp knife; place, 1 inch apart, on greased cookie sheets.
6 Bake in moderate oven (375°) 10 minutes, or until firm. Remove from cookie sheets at once; cool completely on wire racks.

Pistachio Buttons

Bake at 350° for 8 minutes. Makes 16 dozen 1-inch cookies

2 cups sifted all-purpose flour
1 teaspoon baking powder
½ teaspoon salt
½ cup (1 stick) butter or margarine
¾ cup sugar
1 egg
1 teaspoon almond extract
¼ teaspoon vanilla
1 envelope (1 ounce) liquid unsweetened chocolate
⅓ cup finely chopped pistachio nuts
10 drops green food coloring

1 Sift flour, baking powder, and salt onto wax paper.
2 Cream butter or margarine with sugar until fluffy-light in a large bowl; beat in egg, almond extract, and vanilla. Stir in flour mixture, a third at a time, blending well to make a stiff dough. Divide dough in half. Blend chocolate into one half; blend pistachio nuts and green food coloring into remaining half. Chill dough several hours, or overnight, until firm enough to handle. Divide each color into 4 even parts.
3 Roll green dough, one part at a time, into a log 8 inches long on a lightly floured pastry cloth or board; chill. Pat chocolate dough, one part at a time, into a rectangle 3 inches wide and 8 inches long. Roll around a green log; pinch edges to seal, then smooth out. Repeat

with remaining doughs to make 4 rolls in all. Chill the rolls for at least an hour.
4 When ready to bake, slice each roll about ⅛ inch thick; place, ½ inch apart, on greased cookie sheets.
5 Bake in moderate oven (350°) 8 minutes, or until firm but not brown. Remove from cookie sheets; cool.

Chocolate Crisps

Crunchy and not too sweet—and perfect with a glass of milk or cup of tea.
Bake at 350° for 10 minutes. Makes about 5 dozen

1¾ cups sifted all-purpose flour
¼ teaspoon baking soda
½ teaspoon salt
½ cup (1 stick) butter or margarine
¾ cup firmly packed brown sugar
1 egg
1 square unsweetened chocolate, melted
¾ teaspoon vanilla

1 Measure flour, soda, and salt into a sifter.
2 Cream butter or margarine with brown sugar until fluffy in a medium-size bowl; beat in egg, melted chocolate, and vanilla. Sift in flour mixture, blending well to make a soft dough.
3 Shape into 2 long rolls in wax paper; wrap tightly; chill overnight. When ready to bake, slice dough ⅛ inch thick; place on greased cookie sheets.
4 Bake in moderate oven (350°) 10 minutes, or until firm. Remove from cookie sheets; cool completely on wire racks.

Lemon Rounds

Dough keeps perfectly, so you can bake it in small batches, if you wish.
Bake at 375° for 8 minutes. Makes 4 dozen

1½ cups sifted all-purpose flour
½ teaspoon baking soda
½ teaspoon salt
½ cup vegetable shortening
1 cup sugar
1 egg
1 tablespoon lemon juice
2 teaspoons grated lemon rind
½ cup finely chopped pecans

1 Measure flour, soda, and salt into a sifter.
2 Cream shortening with sugar until fluffy in a medium-size bowl; beat in egg, lemon juice and rind, and pecans. Sift in flour mixture, blending well to make a soft dough.
3 Shape into 2 long rolls; wrap in wax paper; chill overnight. When ready to bake, slice dough ¼ inch thick; place on cookie sheets.
4 Bake in moderate oven (375°) 8 minutes, or until golden around edges. Remove from cookie sheets; cool completely on wire racks.

BAR COOKIES

Best-Ever Brownies
"Irresistible" best describes these rich sweets with moist fudgy centers.
Bake at 350° for 30 minutes. Makes 16 squares

2 squares unsweetened chocolate
½ cup (1 stick) butter or margarine
2 eggs
1 cup sugar
½ teaspoon vanilla
½ cup sifted all-purpose flour
⅛ teaspoon salt
1 cup chopped walnuts

1 Melt chocolate with butter or margarine in a small saucepan.
2 Beat eggs until foamy in a large bowl; beat in sugar gradually until fluffy-thick. (This will take about 10 minutes.) Stir in vanilla and chocolate mixture, then fold in flour, salt, and walnuts. Spread in a greased baking pan, 8x8x2.
3 Bake in moderate oven (350°) 30 minutes, or until shiny and firm on top. Cool completely in pan on a wire rack; cut into 2-inch squares.

613

The best of all bar cookies are Best-Ever Brownies (lined up at right). They're the chewy sort of brownie that brownie-lovers love.

Choco-Butterscotch Squares

They're a triple treat with chocolate and walnuts between two chewy butterscotch layers.
Bake at 375° for 40 minutes. Makes 3 dozen

¾ cup sifted all-purpose flour
1 teaspoon salt
½ teaspoon baking soda
½ cup vegetable shortening (for butterscotch layers)
¾ cup firmly packed brown sugar
1 egg
1 teaspoon vanilla
1 cup corn flakes, crushed
1 cup quick-cooking rolled oats
1 package (6 ounces) butterscotch-flavor pieces
1 package (6 ounces) semisweet-chocolate pieces
1 tablespoon vegetable shortening (for chocolate layer)
1 can (4 ounces) walnuts, chopped (1 cup)
⅓ cup sweetened condensed milk (from a 14- or 15-ounce can)

1 Measure flour, salt, and soda into a sifter.
2 Cream the ½ cup shortening with brown sugar until fluffy in a large bowl; beat in egg and vanilla. Sift in flour mixture, blending well to make a soft dough.
3 Stir in crushed corn flakes, rolled oats, and butterscotch-flavor pieces. Spread half of the mixture evenly over bottom of a greased baking pan, 9x9x2; set remaining aside for Step 5.
4 Melt semisweet-chocolate pieces with the 1 tablespoon shortening in top of a double boiler over simmering water; remove from water. Stir in walnuts and sweetened condensed milk.
5 Spread over layer in pan, then spread with remaining butterscotch mixture.
6 Bake in moderate oven (375°) 40 minutes, or until firm and golden. Cool completely in pan on a wire rack. Cut into 36 squares.

Chocolate Trinkets

Part candy and part cookie, they go together and bake fast. Recipe makes lots, too.
Bake at 350° for 15 minutes. Makes about 5 dozen

2 packages (4 ounces each) sweet cooking chocolate

1 cup chopped walnuts
1 egg
½ cup sugar
1 can (3½ ounces) flaked coconut
8 candied red cherries

1 Heat chocolate in a baking pan, 9x9x2, while oven heats, 5 minutes, or just until soft. Spread in an even layer; sprinkle walnuts on top, pressing in lightly.
2 Beat egg until foamy in a small bowl; beat in sugar until well-blended; mix in coconut. Spread evenly on top of chocolate-walnut layer.
3 Cut candied cherries into eighths; place in even rows on top.
4 Bake in moderate oven (350°) 15 minutes, or just until coconut topping is set.
5 Cool in pan on a wire rack; cut into about-1-inch squares, but leave in pan. Chill until ready to serve, then cut again and remove.

Chocolate Shortbread

Bake at 300° for 40 minutes. Makes 8 dozen

1 cup (2 sticks) butter or margarine
½ cup very fine granulated sugar
2 squares semisweet chocolate, melted
2 cups sifted all-purpose flour
 Green decorating frosting from a pressurized can or a tube
 Candied red cherries, slivered

1 Cream butter or margarine with sugar until fluffy-light in a medium-size bowl. Beat in melted chocolate; stir in flour until well-blended.
2 Spread dough evenly in an ungreased baking pan, 13x9x2.
3 Bake in slow oven (300°) 40 minutes, or until firm. Cool slightly in pan on a wire rack, then cut lengthwise into 8 strips and crosswise into 12 to make about-1-inch squares. Cool completely. Decorate each with green frosting and a sliver of candied cherry.

Coffee-Date Bars

They're chewy with dates and nuts and have a pleasingly strong coffee flavor.
Bake at 350° for 35 minutes. Makes 3 dozen bars

1¼ cups sifted all-purpose flour
2 tablespoons instant coffee powder
1 teaspoon baking powder
¼ teaspoon salt

614

3 eggs
1 cup sugar
½ cup finely chopped pitted dates
½ cup coarsely chopped walnuts

1 Measure flour, instant coffee, baking powder, and salt into a sifter.
2 Beat eggs until light in a medium-size bowl; beat in sugar slowly; continue beating until thick, then beat in dates and walnuts. Sift flour mixture over and fold in. Spread in a greased baking pan, 13x9x2.
3 Bake in moderate oven (350°) 35 minutes, or until a wooden pick inserted in center comes out clean. Cool completely in pan on a wire rack; cut into bars.

●

Toffee-Raisin Bars
Lots of sugar, spice, and fruit go into these chewy cookies. They save time on busy days, for they take no fancy shaping.
Bake at 375° for 20 minutes. Makes 30 bars

2 cups sifted all-purpose flour
½ teaspoon baking soda
½ teaspoon ground nutmeg
½ teaspoon ground cinnamon
¼ teaspoon ground cloves
1 cup (2 sticks) butter or margarine
1¼ cups firmly packed brown sugar
2 eggs
2 tablespoons milk
1½ cups raisins

1 Measure flour, soda, nutmeg, cinnamon, and cloves into sifter.
2 Cream butter or margarine with brown sugar until fluffy in large bowl; beat in eggs and milk until well-blended.
3 Sift in dry ingredients, a third at a time, blending well to make a thick batter; stir in raisins. Spread evenly in lightly greased baking pan, 15x10x1.
4 Bake in moderate oven (375°) 20 minutes, or until browned around edges and top springs back when lightly pressed with fingertip. Cool in pan on wire rack; cut into bars or squares. (They're perfect, too, as a dinner dessert topped with sweetened whipped cream or ice cream.)

Date-Nut Chews
Bake 'em, then shape 'em. A little makes a lot.
Bake at 350° for 20 minutes. Makes 12½ dozen

¾ cup sifted all-purpose flour
1 cup sugar
½ teaspoon baking powder
¼ teaspoon salt
1 cup chopped pitted dates
1 cup chopped walnuts
2 eggs
10X (confectioners' powdered) sugar

1 Measure flour, sugar, baking powder, and salt into sifter.
2 Combine dates and walnuts in medium-size bowl; sift dry ingredients over; mix well.
3 Beat eggs until light in small bowl; stir into date-nut mixture; spread thinly in well-buttered baking pan, 15x10x1.
4 Bake in moderate oven (350°) 20 minutes, or until golden-brown.
5 Cool in pan 5 minutes; cut into strips, 1x2 inches; remove, one at a time, and roll into a log shape; slice crosswise into 1-inch-thick pieces; sprinkle with confectioners' (powdered) sugar.

Raspberry Chews
Bake at 350° for 40 minutes. Makes about 8 dozen

¾ cup (1½ sticks) butter or margarine
¾ cup sugar
2 eggs, separated
1½ cups sifted all-purpose flour
1 cup chopped walnuts
1 cup raspberry preserves
½ cup flaked coconut

1 Cream butter or margarine with ¼ cup of the sugar until fluffy-light in a medium-size bowl; beat in egg yolks.
2 Stir in flour until blended. Spread evenly in an ungreased baking pan, 13x9x2.
3 Bake in moderate oven (350°) 15 minutes, or until golden; remove from oven.
4 While layer bakes, beat egg whites until foamy-white and double in volume in a small bowl; beat in remaining ½ cup sugar until meringue stands in firm peaks; fold in walnuts.
5 Spread raspberry preserves over layer in pan; sprinkle with coconut. Spread meringue over raspberry-coconut layer.
6 Bake in moderate oven (350°) 25 minutes, or until lightly golden. Cool completely in pan on a wire rack. Cut into about-1-inch squares.

615

Date Accordions

Bake at 350° for 25 minutes. Makes about 6 dozen

¾ *cup sifted all-purpose flour*
½ *teaspoon baking powder*
¼ *teaspoon salt*
3 *eggs*
1 *cup sugar (for dough)*
2 *tablespoons orange juice*
1 *package (8 ounces) pitted dates, chopped*
1 *cup chopped pecans*
¼ *cup chopped candied orange peel*
   Sugar (for coating)
   Canned or refrigerated ready-to-spread vanilla frosting
   Green decorating gel in plastic tube

1 Sift flour, baking powder, and salt onto wax paper.
2 Beat eggs until foamy-light in a large bowl; slowly beat in the 1 cup sugar; continue beating until mixture is fluffy-thick. Stir in orange juice.
3 Fold in flour mixture, dates, pecans, and orange peel. Spread evenly in a greased baking pan, 13x9x2.
4 Bake in moderate oven (350°) 25 minutes, or until golden and top springs back when lightly pressed with fingertip. Cool in pan on a wire rack 15 minutes.
5 Cut lengthwise into 9 strips and crosswise into 8 to make 72 pieces, about 1x1½. Roll each in sugar in a pie plate to coat generously. (Cookies are soft and will roll into a log.)
6 Top each with an accordion-shape ribbon of vanilla frosting pressed through a pastry tube, then cover frosting with green decorating gel. Let stand on wire racks until frosting is firm.

Coconut Chews

616

Bake at 300° for 30 minutes. Makes 4 dozen

1 *egg*
½ *cup sugar*
1 *teaspoon vanilla*
1 *cup finely chopped pitted dates*
1 *package (7 ounces) cookie coconut*
⅓ *cup finely chopped candied red cherries*
⅓ *cup chopped walnuts*
   Red and green food colorings

1 Beat egg until foamy in a medium-size bowl; beat in sugar until fluffy-thick. Stir in vanilla, dates, ¾ cup of the coconut, cherries, and walnuts. Spoon into a greased baking pan, 9x9x2.
2 Bake in slow oven (300°) 30 minutes, or until golden and top springs back when lightly pressed with fingertip. Cool in pan on a wire rack 15 minutes, or just until warm.
3 While cookies cool, divide remaining coconut into two small jars with lids. Add a drop or two of red or green food colorings to each; shake until coconut is evenly tinted. Spread out on sheets of wax paper.
4 Cut cookies lengthwise into 8 strips and crosswise into 6 to make 48 pieces. Roll each into a ball between palms of hands, then roll in tinted coconut to coat generously. Cool completely on wire racks.

Cranberry Crunch Bars

Bake at 400° for 35 minutes. Makes 8 dozen small bars

1¾ *cups sifted all-purpose flour*
 ¾ *teaspoon salt*
1½ *teaspoons ground cinnamon*
1¼ *cups firmly packed light brown sugar*
 2 *cups quick-cooking rolled oats*
 1 *cup (2 sticks) butter or margarine*
 1 *cup finely chopped walnuts*
 ½ *cup granulated sugar*
 2 *tablespoons cornstarch*
 2 *jars (14 ounces each) cranberry-orange relish*
 1 *egg*
 1 *tablespoon water*
   10X (confectioners' powdered) sugar

1 Sift flour, salt, and cinnamon into a large bowl; stir in brown sugar and rolled oats. Cut in butter or margarine with a pastry blender until mixture is crumbly; stir in walnuts. Press half of mixture evenly over bottom of a lightly greased baking pan, 13x9x2.
2 Bake in hot oven (400°) 5 minutes; cool slightly on a wire rack.
3 While layer bakes, mix granulated sugar and cornstarch in a medium-size saucepan; stir in cranberry relish. Cook slowly, stirring constantly, until mixture thickens and boils 3 minutes. Spread evenly over partly baked layer in pan. Sprinkle remaining rolled-oats mixture over top; press down firmly with hand.
4 Beat egg well in a cup; stir in water. Brush lightly over crumb mixture.
5 Bake in hot oven (400°) 30 minutes, or until firm and golden. Cool completely in pan on a wire rack.

6 Cut in quarters lengthwise, then crosswise; lift each piece from pan with a pancake turner. Cut each of these pieces in half crosswise, then in thirds lengthwise to make 6 small bars. Dust lightly with 10X sugar.

●

Triple-Treat Chews

Layers of orange pastry and nut-filled cookie dough with chocolate between.
Bake at 375° for 30 minutes. Makes 8 dozen

1¾ cups sifted all-purpose flour
1½ cups firmly packed light brown sugar
1 tablespoon grated orange rind
½ teaspoon salt
½ cup (1 stick) butter or margarine
1 package (6 ounces) semisweet-chocolate pieces
2 eggs
½ teaspoon baking powder
1 teaspoon vanilla
1½ cups chopped walnuts

1 Combine 1½ cups of the flour, ½ cup of the brown sugar, orange rind, and ¼ teaspoon of the salt in a large bowl; cut in butter or margarine with a pastry blender until mixture is crumbly. Press evenly over bottom of an ungreased baking pan, 13x9x2, to make a layer.
2 Bake in moderate oven (375°) 10 minutes, or until firm. Remove from oven but leave heat on. Sprinkle chocolate pieces over layer in pan; let stand about 2 minutes, or until chocolate softens; spread evenly over pastry with a knife to make a second layer.
3 Beat eggs until thick in a medium-size bowl; stir in remaining 1 cup brown sugar, ¼ cup flour, ¼ teaspoon salt, baking powder, vanilla, and walnuts. Spread over chocolate layer in pan.
4 Bake 20 minutes longer, or until top is firm and golden. Cool completely in pan on a wire rack. Cut into about-1-inch squares. For a garnish, top each square with a walnut half held in place with a dot of confectioners'-sugar icing.

Lebkuchen Squares

Each sweet and chewy cherry-topped cookie is rich with spice, almonds, and raisins.
Bake at 350° for 30 minutes. Makes 6 dozen

1 cup honey
¾ cup firmly packed brown sugar
1 egg
1 teaspoon grated lemon rind
3 tablespoons lemon juice
2 cups sifted all-purpose flour
1 tablespoon pumpkin-pie spice
½ teaspoon baking soda
¼ teaspoon salt
½ cup golden raisins
½ cup chopped blanched almonds
1 cup sifted 10X (confectioners' powdered) sugar
18 candied green cherries, halved
18 candied red cherries, halved

1 Heat honey to boiling in small saucepan; pour into large bowl; cool completely. Stir in brown sugar, egg, lemon rind, and 1 tablespoon lemon juice. (Save remaining 2 tablespoons for Step 5.)
2 Sift dry ingredients into medium-size bowl; stir in raisins and almonds. Gradually stir into honey mixture, blending well. Chill overnight to blend flavors.
3 Divide dough and spread evenly into 2 greased baking pans, each 9x9x2.
4 Bake in moderate oven (350°) 30 minutes, or until firm.
5 While cookies bake, stir saved 2 tablespoons lemon juice into 10X sugar until smooth in small bowl.
6 Set pans of hot cookies on wire racks; press 36 cherry halves, cut side down, in 6 even rows on top in each pan; drizzle frosting over. Cool cookies completely in pans, then cut each panful into 36 squares.

Walnut Frosties

Cut this triple-layer confection into bitsy squares, for it's rich and sweet.
Bake at 350° for 35 minutes. Makes 3 dozen

1 cup sifted all-purpose flour (for crust)
2 tablespoons 10X (confectioners' powdered) sugar
½ cup (1 stick) butter or margarine
2 eggs
1 cup firmly packed brown sugar
2 tablespoons all-purpose flour (for topping)
½ teaspoon baking powder
⅛ teaspoon salt
1 cup coarsely chopped walnuts
½ cup flaked coconut
ORANGE BUTTER CREAM (recipe follows)

1 Combine 1 cup flour and 10X sugar in me-

617

dium-size bowl; cream in butter or margarine until well-blended. Pat firmly and evenly into bottom of an ungreased baking pan, 9x9x2.

2 Bake in moderate oven (350°) 10 minutes; remove and let cool on wire rack 5 minutes. (Leave oven heat on.)

3 Beat eggs slightly in medium-size bowl; stir in brown sugar until well-blended, then 2 tablespoons flour, baking powder, and salt. Fold in walnuts and coconut; pour over crust.

4 Bake 25 minutes longer, or until top is firm; cool completely in pan. Frost with ORANGE BUTTER CREAM; cut into 36 tiny squares. Top each with a walnut half, if you wish.

ORANGE BUTTER CREAM—Beat 2 tablespoons melted butter or margarine and 1½ teaspoons orange juice into 1¼ cups sifted 10X (confectioners' powdered) sugar until smooth and creamy in small bowl; stir in 1½ teaspoons grated orange rind. Makes about ½ cup.

Royal Scotch Shortbread

A tradition in many homes at Christmas time. Make ahead, for it tastes even richer if mellowed a few weeks.

Bake at 300° for 45 minutes. Makes about 4 dozen

1½ cups sifted all-purpose flour
1½ cups sifted 10X (confectioners' powdered) sugar
1 cup (2 sticks) butter or margarine

1 Sift flour and 10X sugar into medium-size bowl; cut in butter or margarine with pastry blender until mixture is crumbly. Work dough into a ball with hands and knead about 10 minutes.

2 Pat dough into a ¼-inch-thick rectangle, 14x12, on large ungreased cookie sheet; cut into 2-inch diamonds or squares with sharp knife but do not separate cookies.

3 Bake in slow oven (300°) 45 minutes, or until firm and delicately golden.

4 Recut cookies at marks and separate very carefully; remove from cookie sheets. Cool on wire racks. These cookies are very delicate, so handle carefully. Store with wax paper or transparent wrap between layers in container with tight-fitting cover.

618

Frosted Jewel Sticks

Bake at 300° for 2½ hours. Makes about 4 dozen

4 cups HOME CANDIED FRUITS (recipe follows)
2 cans (3 ounces each) pecans, chopped
4 cups sifted all-purpose flour
2 teaspoons baking powder
1½ teaspoons salt
1 cup (2 sticks) butter or margarine
1½ cups sugar
4 eggs
½ cup milk
½ teaspoon almond extract
BASIC BUTTER CREAM (recipe follows)

1 Line a baking pan, 15x10x1, with a double thickness of brown paper; grease paper.

2 Combine candied fruits and pecans in a large bowl.

3 Sift flour, baking powder, and salt onto wax paper; sprinkle 1 cup over fruit mixture; toss lightly.

4 Cream butter or margarine with sugar until fluffy in a large bowl; beat in eggs, 1 at a time. Blend in remaining flour mixture, adding alternately with milk; stir in almond extract, then fold in fruit mixture. Spoon into prepared pan, spreading evenly.

5 Bake in slow oven (300°) 2½ hours, or until a wooden pick inserted in center comes out clean.

6 Let cool completely in pan on a wire rack. Loosen around edge with knife; turn out onto rack; peel off paper. Frost with BASIC BUTTER CREAM and sprinkle with grated semisweet chocolate, if you wish. Cut into sticks, each about 3x1.

BASIC BUTTER CREAM—Cream ½ cup (1 stick) butter or margarine until soft in a medium-size bowl; beat in 1 package (1 pound) 10X (confectioners' powdered) sugar, alternately with mixture of 3 tablespoons milk and 1 teaspoon vanilla until smooth. Makes 2 cups.

Home Candied Fruits

Makes about 4 cups

2 oranges
1 lemon
1 can (1 pound 14 ounces) sliced pineapple
1 jar (8 ounces) maraschino cherries
2 cups golden raisins
1 cup sugar

1 Peel rinds from oranges and lemon in big chunks; simmer in water to cover 15 minutes; drain. Scrape off white membrane; cut the rinds in matchlike strips.

Looking for an absolutely sensational bar cookie fancy enough for a party? Then try showy Peanut Butter Bars.

2 Combine strips with pineapple slices and syrup, cherries (make sure they're well-drained), and the raisins in large frying pan; sprinkle evenly with sugar.

3 Cook, stirring often, 30 minutes, or until glazed. Let stand in syrup overnight; place on a cheesecloth-covered rack; cover. Dry two days, then chop.

Peanut-Butter Bars

These moist chewy bar cookies, drizzled with glaze then with chocolate, will be a favorite with the kids.

Bake at 350° for 35 minutes. Makes three dozen

1 cup crunchy peanut butter
⅔ cup butter or margarine, softened
1 teaspoon vanilla
2 cups firmly packed light brown sugar
3 eggs
1 cup sifted all-purpose flour
½ teaspoon salt
¾ cup sifted 10X (confectioners' powdered) sugar

2 teaspoons water
¼ cup semisweet chocolate pieces (from a 6-ounce package)
1 teaspoon vegetable shortening

1 Combine peanut butter, butter or margarine and vanilla in a large bowl; beat with electric beater until well-blended; beat in sugar until light and fluffy; beat in eggs, one at a time.

2 Stir in flour and salt just until well-blended; spread batter in a greased 13x9x2-inch baking pan.

3 Bake in moderate oven (350°) 35 minutes, or until center springs back when lightly touched with fingertip. Remove pan from oven to wire rack; cool slightly.

4 Combine 10X sugar with water in a small bowl; stir until smooth; drizzle from a spoon over still-warm cookies in pan; swirl with bowl of spoon to make a random pattern.

5 Melt chocolate with shortening over simmering water in top of double boiler. Drizzle over the white glaze for a black-and-white pattern. When cool, using a sharp knife, cut into 36 rectangles. Carefully lift out of pan with spatula.

619

A doubly effective way to cool off in summer, Green Pea Crème, nestled in a bowl of cracked ice, looks every bit as cool as it is.

Another great way to beat the heat is tart-sweet Scandinavian Fruit-Cup Soup.

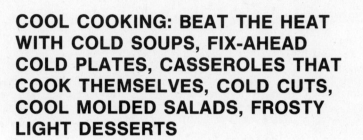

COOL COOKING: BEAT THE HEAT WITH COLD SOUPS, FIX-AHEAD COLD PLATES, CASSEROLES THAT COOK THEMSELVES, COLD CUTS, COOL MOLDED SALADS, FROSTY LIGHT DESSERTS

When temperatures soar and energies plummet, who wants to stand over a hot stove? No one, obviously. But no one *needs* to. It's possible to prepare three square (three *smashing*) meals a day and keep cool at the same time. Magic? Not really. It's more a matter of common sense. For example, make the most of cold cuts, cheeses, canned and convenience foods that require little or no cooking . . . when you *do* cook, cook in the cool of the day, preparing enough at one time to last two or more meals . . . for that one hot dish (if the family insists), choose a casserole that practically cooks itself . . . but most of the time, concentrate on cool gelatin salads (loaded with meat, poultry or fish) and concoct frosty, shimmery desserts. You'll keep cool psychologically as well as physically.

BEAT THE HEAT WITH— COLD SOUPS

Jellied Avocado Soup
A twin to popular guacamole, it has the same peppy flavor.
Makes 6 servings

   1 envelope unflavored gelatin
   1 teaspoon salt
   1 teaspoon sugar
   1 teaspoon chili powder
   1 envelope instant chicken broth
     OR: 1 chicken-bouillon cube
1½ cups water
   1 large ripe avocado
   2 tablespoons lemon juice
   1 teaspoon grated onion
   1 cup (8-ounce carton) dairy sour cream
   2 tablespoons mayonnaise or salad dressing
   3 small firm ripe tomatoes, peeled and diced

1 Mix gelatin with salt, sugar, and chili powder in a small saucepan; add chicken broth or bouillon cube; stir in water.
2 Heat slowly, stirring constantly, until gelatin and bouillon cube, if used, dissolve. Let cool while preparing avocado.
3 Halve avocado; peel and pit. Press avocado through coarse sieve into a medium-size bowl; stir in lemon juice, onion, sour cream, and mayonnaise or salad dressing. Beat in gelatin mixture until smooth. Pour into a pan, 8x8x2. Chill several hours, or until firm.
4 When ready to serve, cut firm avocado mixture into large cubes; layer cubes and diced tomato, alternately, into parfait glasses. Garnish with watercress, if you wish.

●

Green Pea Créme
So cool and refreshing and it goes together quickly with frozen peas.
Makes 6 servings

1 package (10 ounces) frozen green peas
1 teaspoon salt
2 cups water
1 envelope instant chicken broth
  OR: 1 chicken-bouillon cube
1 cup cream for whipping
1 tablespoon chopped fresh mint
  OR: ½ teaspoon dried mint leaves, crushed
1 teaspoon grated onion
⅛ teaspoon liquid red pepper seasoning

1 Combine peas, salt, and 1 cup of the water in a small saucepan; cook 5 minutes, or until peas are tender. Stir in chicken broth or bouillon cube until dissolved.
2 Pour into an electric-blender container; cover; beat until smooth. (If you do not have a blender, press mixture through a sieve into a medium-size bowl.)
3 Stir in remaining 1 cup water, cream, mint, onion, and red pepper seasoning. Chill well.
4 Ladle into small bowls or glass cups; garnish each with a sprig of fresh mint, if you wish.

Tomato Frappé
Its piquant flavor starts any meal right—and your blender does the work.
Makes 6 generous servings

1 can (1 pound) tomatoes
¼ cup olive oil or vegetable oil
2 tablespoons lemon juice
1 tablespoon sugar
1 tablespoon seasoned salt
1 teaspoon Worcestershire sauce
1 small cucumber, pared, cut up, and seeded
1 medium-size carrot, pared and sliced
1 large stalk celery, trimmed and sliced
1 can (46 ounces) mixed vegetable juice

1 Combine tomatoes, olive oil or vegetable oil, lemon juice, sugar, seasoned salt, and Worcestershire sauce in an electric-blender container. Beat until smooth; pour into a large bowl.
2 Combine cucumber, carrot, celery, and 1 cup of the mixed vegetable juice in blender container; beat until smooth. Stir into tomato mixture in bowl with remaining mixed vegetable juice. Chill thoroughly.
3 When ready to serve, pour into small cups or bowls; garnish each with a thin strip of green pepper and several small onion rings, if you

622

wish. (Any left? Store in a covered jar in the refrigerator.)

●

Jellied Madrilène Seville
No one will ever guess the surprise ingredient—it's popular cola.
Makes 4 servings

1 envelope unflavored gelatin
1 can (about 13 ounces) condensed consommé madrilène
1 bottle (about 7 ounces) cola beverage
½ teaspoon grated orange rind
2 tablespoons lemon juice
¼ teaspoon bottled aromatic bitters
1 small seedless orange, cut in 4 wedges

1 Soften gelatin in consommé madrilène in a medium-size saucepan; heat slowly, stirring constantly, until gelatin dissolves; remove from heat. Stir in cola beverage, orange rind, lemon juice, and bitters.
2 Pour into a pan, 9x9x2; chill several hours, or until firm.
3 When ready to serve, cut gelatin in ½-inch cubes with a sharp knife. Spoon into small glass bowls or cups. Serve each with an orange wedge to squeeze over top.

●

Tuna Bisque
Potato soup mix is the base for this mellow dinner starter.
Makes 6 servings

1 envelope (3 ounces) potato soup mix
2 cups water
1 cup milk
1 cup light cream or table cream
1 can (about 4 ounces) tuna, drained and chopped fine
  Paprika

1 Prepare potato soup mix with water and milk, following label directions; pour into a large bowl.
2 Stir in light cream and chopped tuna. Chill well.
3 Ladle into small cups or bowls; sprinkle with paprika.

Apple Vichyssoise
A secret ingredient gives this variation of a classic such a fresh flavor.
Makes 6 servings

As sparkly as a mini-mountain of topazes, cooling Jellied Madrilène Seville made with a cola drink.

1 can (10¼ ounces) frozen cream of potato
   soup, thawed
1½ cups milk
1 cup cream for whipping
⅓ cup unsweetened applesauce
   Salt
   Chopped watercress

1 Combine soup and milk in an electric-blender container; cover; beat until smooth. (If you do not have a blender, press soup through a sieve into a medium-size bowl, then combine with milk.) Stir in ½ cup of the cream and applesauce. Chill well.
2 Just before serving, beat remaining ½ cup cream with salt until stiff in a small bowl.
3 Pour soup into small cups or bowls; top each with a spoonful of whipped cream and sprinkle with chopped watercress.

Scandinavian Fruit-Cup Soup
Try it, too, as a light ending for summery meals. Fruits can be varied with whatever you have on hand.
Makes 6 servings

3 tablespoons tapioca
2 tablespoons sugar
   Dash of salt

2½ cups water
1 can (6 ounces) frozen concentrated pineapple-orange juice
2 firm ripe peaches, peeled, pitted, and sliced
1 cup fresh raspberries
1 tablespoon lemon juice

1 Combine tapioca, sugar, and salt in a small saucepan; stir in 1 cup of the water. Heat, stirring constantly, to a full rolling boil; pour into a medium-size bowl.
2 Stir in frozen pineapple-orange juice until melted, then remaining 1½ cups water. Chill well. (Mixture will thicken slightly.)
3 Just before serving, stir in prepared fruits and lemon juice.
4 Ladle into small glass bowls or cups.

Summer Garden Soup
A favorite with a twist. Crisp vegetables are folded into fast-fix onion soup.
Makes 6 servings

623

1 can or 1 envelope (1⅜ ounces) onion soup
   mix
3 cups water
2 firm ripe tomatoes, peeled and chopped
1 large cucumber, pared, seeded, and finely
   chopped
1 sweet red pepper, halved, seeded, and finely
   chopped

1 Prepare onion soup mix with the 3 cups water, following label directions; pour into a large bowl. Chill well.

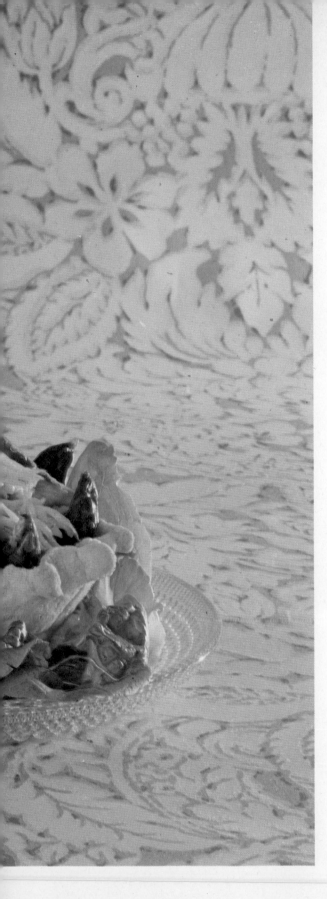

2 Just before serving, stir in tomatoes, cucumber, and red pepper.
3 Ladle into small bowls or cups; float a thin slice of cucumber on top, if you wish.

BEAT THE HEAT WITH—
FIX-AHEAD COLD PLATES

Rainbow Turkey Tray
A frozen boneless turkey roast costars with summer-bright fruits for this meal-in-one.
Roast at 400° for 2 hours. Makes 6 servings

1 packaged frozen boneless turkey roast, weighing about 2 pounds
  ORANGE-SPICE DRESSING (recipe follows)
  APRICOT CREAMS (recipe follows)
1 pint strawberries (2 cups)
1 cup blueberries
  Escarole

1 Roast frozen turkey in its foil package, following label directions; remove from package; chill. (Meat slices neater when allowed to chill completely, so you can roast it a day ahead, if you wish.)
2 Make ORANGE-SPICE DRESSING; chill.
3 When ready to arrange platter, make APRICOT CREAMS; wash strawberries and hull; wash blueberries and stem.
4 Line a large shallow tray with escarole; arrange strawberries in a mound in center.
5 Carve turkey into ¼-inch-thick slices; place, overlapping and alternating light and dark ends of slices, on tray.
6 Arrange APRICOT CREAMS around turkey; spoon blueberries around apricots. Serve with ORANGE-SPICE DRESSING

625

Orange-Spice Dressing
Cardamom and fruit are such refreshing flavor mates.
Makes about ⅔ cup

⅓ cup vegetable oil
¼ cup orange juice

Left to right: Rainbow Turkey Tray, Tomato Aspic Miniatures served in tomatoes, Crab Louis Pielets.

2 tablespoons lemon juice
¼ teaspoon salt
    Dash of cardamom

Combine all ingredients in a jar with a tight-fitting cover; shake well to mix. Chill.

●

Apricot Creams
Always a delicacy, this fresh golden fruit is filled with tangy sour cream.
Makes 6 servings

6 fresh apricots
¼ cup dairy sour cream
2 tablespoons chopped walnuts

1 Halve apricots; remove seeds.
2 Blend sour cream and walnuts in a cup; spoon into hollows in apricots. Chill until serving time.

Buffet Beef Plates
Meat, tomato molds, and cucumber relishes can be fixed a day early, ready to arrange with warm spinach salad just before mealtime.
Roast at 325° for 2 hours. Makes enough for 2 meals, 6 servings each

1 eye-round or sirloin beef roast, weighing
    about 3 pounds
1 teaspoon seasoned salt
¼ teaspoon seasoned pepper
    TOMATO ASPIC MINIATURES (recipe follows)
    CUCUMBER PINWHEELS (recipe follows)
3 large firm ripe tomatoes
¼ large cucumber, cut in 6 thin slices
    SPINACH HOLLANDIA (recipe follows)

1 Sprinkle roast with seasoned salt and pepper; place on a rack in a shallow baking pan. If using a meat thermometer, insert bulb into thickest part of roast.
2 Roast in slow oven (325°) 2 hours, or until thermometer registers 140° for rare, or 160° for medium. Cool, then wrap and chill until ready to serve.
3 Make TOMATO ASPIC MINIATURES and CUCUM-BER PINWHEELS; chill both.
4 When ready to serve, halve tomatoes cross-wise. (To make a fancy fluted edge, mark a guideline around middle of each tomato with wooden picks, then make even saw-tooth cuts into tomato above and below line, cutting through to center. Pull halves apart gently.) Place tomatoes on individual serving plates; top each with a slice of cucumber and a TOMATO ASPIC MINIATURE.
5 Cut 12 thin slices from chilled roast; roll up each; place 2 on each plate. (Wrap remaining roast and keep chilled for another day.) Place CUCUMBER PINWHEELS alongside.
6 Make SPINACH HOLLANDIA; spoon around tomatoes.

●

Cucumber Pinwheels
Simple cutting trick and an egg-salad filling turn cucumber into these fancies.
Makes 6 servings

1 large cucumber
2 hard-cooked eggs, shelled
2 tablespoons chopped watercress
1 tablespoon mayonnaise or salad dressing
½ teaspoon salt
½ teaspoon dry mustard
½ teaspoon Worcestershire sauce

1 Pare cucumber; cut into 2-inch lengths. Working with one piece at a time and holding it upright, insert a small sharp knife about ⅛ inch in from edge, then cut round and round to seedy center; discard center. (After cutting, you should be able to unroll cucumber into a rectangle.)
2 Chop eggs into a medium-size bowl; stir in watercress, mayonnaise or salad dressing, salt, mustard, and Worcestershire sauce.
3 Carefully unroll cucumber pieces and spread inside of each with egg mixture; reroll tightly. Wrap each in transparent wrap; chill several hours.
4 Cut into ¼-inch-thick slices with a sharp knife.

Spinach Hollandia
Bacon-vinegar dressing seasons freshly cooked spinach for this warm salad.
Makes 6 servings

2 packages (10 ounces each) fresh spinach
4 slices bacon, diced
2 tablespoons wine vinegar or cider vinegar
¾ teaspoon salt
¼ teaspoon pepper

1 Remove any coarse outer leaves and stems

626

from spinach; wash leaves well; drain. Pile into a large frying pan. (No need to add water.) Cover.

2 Heat to boiling, then steam 3 minutes, or just until leaves wilt; drain well.

3 While spinach cooks, sauté bacon until crisp in a small frying pan; drain on paper toweling. Remove frying pan from heat; pour off all drippings, then measure 3 tablespoonfuls back into pan.

4 Stir in vinegar, salt, and pepper; pour over drained spinach; add bacon and toss lightly to coat well.

Tomato Aspic Miniatures

Chopped tomato is molded into gelatin for these double-good salads.
Makes 6 servings

    1 package (3 ounces) lemon-flavor gelatin
1¼ cups hot tomato juice
    3 tablespoons cider vinegar
    1 medium-size firm ripe tomato, peeled and
       chopped
    1 cup chopped celery

1 Dissolve gelatin in hot tomato juice in a medium-size bowl; stir in vinegar. Chill 50 minutes, or until as thick as unbeaten egg white.

2 Fold in chopped tomato and celery; spoon into 6 individual molds or 4-ounce custard cups. Chill several hours, or until firm.

3 When ready to serve, unmold onto serving plates.

Crab Louis Pielets

Each little shell holds crunchy crab salad framed with zippy-seasoned asparagus.
Bake tart shells at 425° for 15 minutes. Makes 6 servings

1 package piecrust mix
2 packages (10 ounces each) frozen asparagus
   spears
1 tablespoon bottled oil-and-vinegar dressing
3 cans (about 7 ounces each) crabmeat
1 can (5 ounces) water chestnuts, drained and
   chopped
  LOUIS DRESSING (recipe follows)
2 heads Bibb lettuce, washed and dried
1 lime, cut into 12 thin slices

1 Prepare piecrust mix, following label direc-

tions. Roll out, half at a time, ⅛ inch thick, on a lightly floured pastry cloth or board; cut each into 3 six-inch rounds, using a saucer for pattern. Fit into 4-inch tart-shell pans, pressing firmly against bottoms and sides; trim overhang to ½ inch; turn under, flush with rim; flute edge. Prick well all over with a fork.

2 Bake in hot oven (425°) 15 minutes, or until golden; cool completely in pans on a wire rack, then remove carefully.

3 Cook asparagus, following label directions; drain. Cut off head of each spear about 1½ inches down; place heads in a pie plate; drizzle with oil-and-vinegar dressing; chill. Cut remaining asparagus stalks in ½-inch-long pieces; place in a medium-size bowl.

4 Drain crabmeat; set aside a few large pieces for garnish, then flake remaining, removing bony tissue, if any. Add with water chestnuts to asparagus in bowl.

5 Make LOUIS DRESSING; spoon 2 tablespoons over crab mixture; toss lightly to mix; chill.

6 When ready to serve, line 6 individual serving plates with lettuce. Stand asparagus spears around edges in tart shells; spoon crab mixture in centers; place on plates. Garnish each tartlet with saved pieces of crab and 2 slices of lime, twisted. Serve with remaining LOUIS DRESSING to spoon over.

LOUIS DRESSING—Blend ½ cup mayonnaise or salad dressing, ½ cup dairy sour cream, ¼ cup catsup, 3 tablespoons chopped green onion, 1 teaspoon sugar, 1 tablespoon lime juice, and a few drops liquid red pepper seasoning in a small bowl; chill. Makes about 1½ cups.

Polynesian Pork

Two salads—curried pork and rice—contrast delightfully with juicy cantaloupe
Roast at 325° about 2½ hours. Makes 6 servings

    1 boned rolled pork shoulder roast, weighing
       about 3 pounds
    1 cup uncooked regular rice
    ½ cup chopped sweet green pepper
    ¼ cup chopped sweet red pepper
    2 tablespoons chopped parsley
    3 tablespoons vegetable oil
    2 tablespoons lemon juice
    2 teaspoons sugar
    1 teaspoon seasoned salt
    2 cups sliced celery
1½ cups mayonnaise or salad dressing
    1 teaspoon curry powder
    1 tablespoon soy sauce
    1 small cantaloupe

627

1 Place roast on a rack in a shallow baking pan. If using a meat thermometer, insert bulb into center of roast.

2 Roast in slow oven (325°) 2½ hours, or until thermometer registers 185°. Cool completely.

3 While meat roasts, cook rice, following label directions. Combine with green and red peppers and parsley in a large bowl. Mix vegetable oil, lemon juice, sugar, and seasoned salt in a cup; pour over rice; toss lightly to mix; chill.

4 Trim all fat from cooled pork, then cut meat into ½-inch cubes; combine with celery in a large bowl. Mix mayonnaise or salad dressing, curry powder, and soy sauce in a 2-cup measure; pour over meat mixture; toss to mix well. Chill.

5 When ready to serve, pile pork salad in center of a large round platter; spoon rice salad around edge.

6 Halve cantaloupe; scoop out seeds. Cut cantaloupe into wedges; pare each; arrange in a ring around pork.

Neptune's Tower

It's amazing how fast you can build this spectacular with ready-seasoned canned and packaged foods.
Makes 8 servings

1 jar (1 pound) pickled green beans
1 can (about 1 pound) green peas with onions
1 can (1 pound) sliced carrots
1 can (about 8 ounces) salmon
1 can (about 7 ounces) tuna
1 can (about 6 ounces) lobster meat
1 can (5 ounces) deveined shrimps
1 jar (12 ounces) olive salad
1 head iceberg lettuce
2 containers (1 pound each) prepared potato salad

628

1 Drain liquid from beans into a cup; set beans aside for step 5. Drain peas and carrots; place in separate small bowls; drizzle each with half of the saved bean liquid; set aside for Step 3.

2 Drain salmon, tuna, and lobster; drain and rinse shrimps. Break salmon and tuna into large chunks. Set aside a few pieces of lobster meat and 1 or 2 shrimps for a garnish, then dice remaining.

3 Drain olive salad, cut up any large pieces. Drain peas and carrots.

4 Break lettuce into bite-size pieces; place in a layer on a shallow large serving platter.

5 Layer remaining foods, building up to a pyramid shape, on top of lettuce this way: Potato salad; peas; tuna, salmon, diced lobster and shrimps; olive salad; carrots; beans. Garnish with saved lobster, shrimps, watercress, and serve with mayonnaise or salad dressing, if you wish.

●

Lazy-Susan Chef's Salad

Set out big bowls so everyone can toss his own to suit his taste.
Makes 8 servings

1 package (12 ounces) assorted sliced cold cuts
1 package (8 ounces) sliced Swiss cheese
1 package (8 ounces) sliced caraway cheese
1 package (8 ounces) sliced process American cheese
1 large red onion, peeled, sliced, and separated into rings
1 bunch radishes, washed and trimmed
1 large cucumber, halved and sliced thin
1 package (about 4 ounces) garlic-flavor croutons
2 small heads romaine, washed and dried
GARLIC DRESSING (recipe follows)

1 Slice cold cuts and cheeses into thin strips. Arrange with onion, radishes, cucumber, and croutons in separate dishes on a Lazy Susan, or pile in separate mounds on a large serving platter.

2 Break romaine into bite-size pieces; place in another bowl in the center.

3 Serve with GARLIC DRESSING.

GARLIC DRESSING—Combine 1 cup olive oil or vegetable oil, ½ cup wine vinegar or cider vinegar, 1 clove garlic, minced, and a dash each of salt and pepper in a small jar with a tight-fitting cover; shake well to mix. Shake again before serving. Makes 1½ cups.

Smorgasbord

Here's how to bring the fun of eating Scandinavian style to your table with little effort.
Makes 8 servings

2 cans (1 pound each) whole potatoes, drained
2 tablespoons bottled oil-and-vinegar dressing

1 jar (12 ounces) herring in sour cream
1 can (about 4 ounces) Vienna sausages, drained
¼ teaspoon dillweed
1 jar (12 ounces) pickled beets, drained
1 jar (1 quart) sauerkraut salad, drained
1 pepperoni (from a 5-ounce package), sliced thin
1 package (6 ounces) sliced boiled ham
1 package (6 ounces) sliced cervelat
1 package (6 ounces) smoked Swiss cheese, sliced thin
1 package (6 ounces) sliced head cheese
1 loaf pumpernickel, buttered

1 Dice potatoes; toss with oil-and-vinegar dressing in a large bowl.
2 Drain creamy liquid from herring into potato bowl; dice herring and Vienna sausages; add to potatoes with dillweed; toss all again. Spoon into a large serving bowl; arrange beets around edge.
3 Place sauerkraut salad in a large shallow bowl. Set both bowls at the edge of a large tray.
4 Arrange pepperoni, ham, cervelat, and cheese in pretty patterns in front of salad bowls; cut head cheese in small squares without separating slices; mound in another pile. Tuck sprigs of parsley between meats and cheeses, if you wish, and serve with pumpernickel.

Barbecued Chicken Supper Salad
Ready-cooked meat and salad come from your supermarket; you add the creative touch.
Makes 4 servings

2 containers (1 pound each) prepared macaroni salad
1 package (4 ounces) shredded Cheddar cheese
1 can (8 ounces) lima beans, drained
½ cup chopped celery
½ teaspoon fines herbes
1 small head chicory, washed, dried, and separated into leaves
2 medium-size tomatoes, cut in wedges
2 ready-to-eat barbecued chickens, weighing about 2 pounds each
  Sweet mixed pickles
  Stuffed green olives

1 Combine macaroni salad, cheese, lima beans, celery, and herbes in a large bowl; toss lightly to mix well. Chill at least an hour to season.

2 Just before serving, line a large platter with chicory leaves; break remaining into bite-size pieces in center; spoon macaroni salad on top. Tuck tomato wedges around salad.
3 Cut chickens in half with kitchen scissors; place, skin side up, around edge of platter.
4 Thread pickles and olives, alternately, onto wooden picks; stick, kebab style, into macaroni salad. Serve with rye-bread-and-butter sandwiches, if you wish.

Oven Beef Bake
Popular ground meat blends with carrots, mushrooms, and macaroni.
Bake at 350° for 1 hour. Makes 8 servings

1 package (8 ounces) elbow macaroni
1 can (1 pound) sliced carrots
1 can (6 ounces) sliced mushrooms
2 pounds ground beef
1 medium-size onion, chopped (½ cup)
2 cups thinly sliced celery
4 tablespoons (½ stick) butter or margarine
5 tablespoons all-purpose flour
1 teaspoon salt
¼ teaspoon pepper
1 can (10½ ounces) condensed beef broth

1 Cook macaroni, following label directions; drain.
2 Drain liquids from carrots and mushrooms into a 4-cup measure and set aside for Step 5. Combine vegetables with macaroni in a greased 12-cup baking dish.
3 Shape ground beef into a patty in a medium-size frying pan; brown 5 minutes on each side, then break up into small chunks. Stir into vegetable mixture in baking dish.
4 Sauté onion and celery in butter or margarine until golden in same frying pan; sprinkle with flour, salt, and pepper, then stir in. Cook, stirring constantly, just until bubbly.
5 Combine beef broth with saved vegetable juices; add water, if needed, to make 3 cups; stir into onion mixture. Continue cooking and stirring until sauce thickens and boils 1 minute. Pour over meat and vegetables; cover.
6 Bake in moderate oven (350°) 1 hour, or until sauce is bubbly. Garnish with rings of green pepper or about a cup of finely shredded lettuce, if you wish.

Veal Risotto
Rice and meat are lightly seasoned with curry for this inviting one-dish meal.
Bake at 350° for 1 hour. Makes 8 servings

629

2 pounds cubed veal shoulder
2 tablespoons vegetable oil
1 tablespoon curry powder
2 cups uncooked regular rice
2 packages (10 ounces each) frozen mixed vegetables
2 tablespoons instant minced onion
2 envelopes instant chicken broth
1½ teaspoons salt
5 cups water
2 canned whole pimientos, drained and halved

1 Trim any fat from veal; brown cubes in vegetable oil in a large frying pan. Stir in curry powder; cook, stirring constantly, 1 minute.
2 While meat browns, mix rice, frozen vegetables, and onion in a greased 12-cup baking dish. Arrange meat in a single layer on top.
3 Stir chicken broth, salt, and water into same frying pan; heat to boiling; pour over meat and vegetables; cover.
4 Bake in moderate oven (350°) 1 hour, or until meat and rice are tender and liquid is absorbed. Arrange pimientos on top.

Chicken Fiesta
Ready-creamed frozen onions and canned soup make the savory sauce in a hurry.
Bake at 350° for 1½ hours. Makes 8 servings

1 package (8 ounces) medium noodles
1 package (9 ounces) frozen onions in cream sauce
2 cans (10½ ounces each) condensed golden mushroom soup

1 package (10 ounces) frozen green peas
4 chicken breasts (about 12 ounces each)

1 Cook noodles, following label directions; drain. Combine with onions and 1 can of the mushroom soup in a greased shallow 12-cup baking dish; sprinkle with peas.
2 While noodles cook, pull skin from chicken breasts; cut each in half. Arrange in a single layer over peas; spread with remaining can of soup; cover.
3 Bake in moderate oven (350°) 1½ hours, or until chicken is tender and sauce is bubbly. Garnish with chopped pistachio nuts, if you wish.

Dixie Chicken Dinner
Meat bakes crispy brown atop layers of beans and olives and tomatoes.
Bake at 350° for 1 hour. Makes 8 servings

2 broiler-fryers, weighing about 2 pounds each
¾ cup sifted all-purpose flour
2 teaspoons salt
1 teaspoon leaf basil, crumbled
4 tablespoons vegetable oil
2 cans (1 pound each) cooked dried lima beans
1 can (1 pound) cut green beans, drained
½ cup sliced stuffed green olives
½ cup sliced pitted ripe olives
4 medium-size firm ripe tomatoes, sliced ½ inch thick
1 clove garlic, minced
½ cup apple juice or water

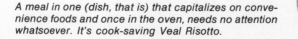

A meal in one (dish, that is) that capitalizes on convenience foods and once in the oven, needs no attention whatsoever. It's cook-saving Veal Risotto.

Lazy-Susan Supper Tray puts a colorful collection of summer favorites on a giant help-yourself turntable.

1 Cut chicken into serving-size pieces. Shake pieces with a mixture of ½ cup of the flour, salt, and basil in a paper bag to coat evenly.

2 Brown slowly in vegetable oil in a large frying pan 10 minutes on each side; remove and set aside.

3 While chicken browns, drain liquid from lima beans into a 2-cup measure; combine limas with green beans, and green and ripe olives in a greased 12-cup shallow baking dish. Place tomato slices in a single layer over vegetables.

4 Pour all drippings from frying pan, then measure 4 tablespoonfuls and return to pan; stir in remaining ¼ cup flour and garlic; cook, stirring constantly, until bubbly.

5 Combine apple juice with saved bean liquid and additional water to make 2 cups; stir into flour mixture in frying pan. Continue cooking and stirring until sauce thickens and boils 1 minute; pour over vegetables in baking dish. Arrange browned chicken in a single layer on top, then press pieces down into vegetables slightly.

6 Bake in moderate oven (350°) 1 hour, or until chicken is tender and sauce bubbles up. Sprinkle with chopped parsley, if you wish.

BEAT THE HEAT WITH— COLD CUTS AND CHEESE

Lazy-Susan Supper Tray

Make up the TRIPLE CHEESE MOLD and TOP-HAT STUFFED EGGS *(recipes follow)* ahead and chill; then you can go as simple or as fancy as you wish in arranging your tray. For interest and variety, use several kinds of cold cuts and cheeses. Our picture shows slices of boiled ham and cheese folded together, along with a pile of bologna and salami rounds. Several thin slices of smoked pressed turkey (buy it in a package) wrapped together make the flower-shape pretties on the top tier. Filling in are tomato slices topped with onion rings in a lettuce nest, and cooked asparagus seasoned with French dressing and bundled inside triangles of sliced spiced ham. For a cool fruit touch, we added crescents of pared honeydew, but you can also use cantaloupe or papaya, if you wish. And don't forget your favorite spreads and rolls. (Our picture shows mayonnaise or salad dressing and prepared mustard in green- and red-pepper cups.)

631

Top-Hat Stuffed Eggs

Gherkin slices perch jauntily on top to make the "hat".
Makes 6 servings

    6 eggs
    ½ cup finely chopped celery
    ¼ cup mayonnaise or salad dressing
    1 tablespoon sweet-pickle juice
    ½ teaspoon salt
    ¼ teaspoon dry mustard
      Dash of pepper
    2 gherkins, sliced

1 Hard-cook and shell eggs. Halve each lengthwise; scoop out yolks and mash in a small bowl.
2 Stir in celery, mayonnaise or salad dressing, pickle juice, salt, dry mustard, and pepper.
3 Pile mixture into whites, dividing evenly; garnish each with a gherkin slice.

Triple Cheese Mold

Mild cream and American cheeses, plus zesty Roquefort, blend in this fluffy spread.
Makes 6 servings

    1 envelope unflavored gelatin
    ¾ cup water
    2 teaspoons Worcestershire sauce
    2 teaspoons lemon juice
    ⅛ teaspoon salt
    1 package (3 or 4 ounces) cream cheese
    2 tablespoons crumbled Roquefort cheese
    2 tablespoons grated process American cheese
    ⅓ cup milk
    2 tablespoons finely chopped green pepper
    ½ teaspoon grated onion
    ½ cup cream for whipping

632

1 Soften gelatin in water in a small saucepan; heat slowly, stirring constantly, just until gelatin dissolves; remove from heat. Stir in Worcestershire sauce, lemon juice, and salt. Cool while blending cheese mixture.
2 Blend cream, Roquefort, and American cheeses in a medium-size bowl; beat in milk until smooth. Stir in cooled gelatin mixture, then green pepper and onion. Chill 20 minutes, or until as thick as unbeaten egg white.
3 Beat cream until stiff in a small bowl; fold into cheese mixture until no streaks of white remain. Spoon into a 3-cup mold. Chill several hours, or until firm.

4 Just before serving, run a sharp-tip thin-blade knife around top of mold, then dip mold *very quickly* in and out of a pan of hot water. Invert onto serving plate; carefully lift off mold. To make a pretty garnish, thread several thin slices of radish, overlapping slightly like petals, on a wooden pick; stick a small pickled onion on top.

Patio Rice Platter

Snowy rice, green onions, and peas in a curry dressing make a handsome mold to serve with sliced tongue or ham.
Makes 8 servings

    2 cups packaged precooked rice (from an about-14-ounce package)
    ¼ cup thin French dressing
    1 package (10 ounces) frozen green peas
    1 cup diced celery
    ½ cup sliced green onions
    ¾ cup mayonnaise or salad dressing
    1 teaspoon curry powder
    ¼ teaspoon salt
    1 pound sliced smoked tongue or ham
      Lettuce
      Ripe olives

1 Prepare rice, following label directions. Place in a large bowl; drizzle French dressing over; toss lightly to mix. Let stand at least an hour to season and blend flavors. (No need to chill, for salad tastes best at room temperature.)
2 Cook peas, following label directions; drain; add to rice mixture with celery and onions.
3 Mix mayonnaise or salad dressing, curry powder, and salt in a 1-cup measure; spoon over rice mixture; toss to mix. Spoon into an 8-cup bowl or mold; press down lightly with back of spoon to make top even; let stand a few minutes.
4 Cover bowl or mold with large serving platter; turn upside down; lift off bowl. Arrange slices of tongue or ham on lettuce leaves around rice; garnish with ripe olives.

Italian Bean Bowl

Men will go for this hearty salad with its zippy seasoned beans and chick peas, plus julienne cold cuts.
Makes 4 to 6 servings

    1 envelope Italian salad-dressing mix
      Red wine vinegar
      Olive oil
    1 package (10 ounces) frozen Italian green beans, cooked and drained

1 can (about 1 pound) chick peas, drained
1 medium-size red onion, chopped
1 small head of lettuce
1 package (6 ounces) Italian assortment sliced
   cold cuts, cut into julienne strips

1 Prepare salad-dressing mix with vinegar, olive oil, and water, following label directions.
2 Combine green beans, chick peas, and onion in a medium-size bowl; drizzle ¼ cup salad dressing over; toss lightly to mix. Let stand at least an hour to season and blend flavors. (Save remaining salad dressing for salad for another meal.)
3 When ready to serve, partly fill a salad bowl with lettuce; spoon bean mixture on top; add meat; toss lightly to mix well.

●

Glazed Bologna Steaks

Like cold cuts hot? Buy meat in a chunk, then slice and bake with a smacking-good maple-flavor sauce.
Bake at 375° for 30 minutes. Makes 6 servings

1 piece bologna, weighing about 1 pound
1 small onion, chopped (¼ cup)
¼ cup blended maple syrup
1 tablespoon lemon juice

1 Cut away casing from bologna; score bologna in diamonds about ½ inch deep, then cut into 6 slices. (This keeps slices from curling.)
2 Place slices in a single layer in a baking dish, 10x6x2; sprinkle with onion; drizzle syrup and lemon juice over.
3 Bake in moderate oven (375°) 30 minutes, or until meat is glazed.

BEAT THE HEAT WITH— COOL MOLDED SALADS

Shrimp-Cucumber Diadem

It's a refreshingly cool two-layer salad with a sparkling crown. Serve with marinated shrimps and hot rolls.
Makes 6 servings

Shrimp Layer

1 bag (1½ pounds) frozen, deveined, shelled, raw shrimps
3 tablespoons bottled Italian-style salad dressing
1 tablespoon chopped parsley
1 envelope unflavored gelatin
2 envelopes instant chicken broth
   OR: 2 envelopes instant vegetable broth
2 cups water
1 teaspoon grated onion
   Few drops liquid red pepper seasoning
1 large cucumber

Cucumber Layer

1 package (3 ounces) lime-flavor gelatin
1 teaspoon salt
1 cup hot water
2 tablespoons cider vinegar
1 cup dairy sour cream
¼ cup mayonnaise or salad dressing
TOMATO TOPPERS (recipe follows)

1 Make shrimp layer: Cook shrimps, following label directions; drain. Set aside about 12 for Step 5. Place remaining in a medium-size bowl; add Italian dressing and parsley; toss lightly. Cover and chill until serving time.

Shrimp-Cucumber Diadem

633

2 Soften unflavored gelatin with chicken or vegetable broth in 1 cup of the water in a medium-size saucepan; heat, stirring constantly, just until gelatin dissolves. Stir in remaining 1 cup water, onion, and red-pepper seasoning. Let stand at room temperature for layering mold in Step 5.

3 Score cucumber rind with a fork for about a quarter of its length, then slice scored part *very thin* and halve each slice. Set aside for making fancy topping in Step 5. Pare remainder of the cucumber; chop—seeds and all—then measure. (There should be about 1¼ cups to use in cucumber layer in Step 6.)

4 Start cucumber layer: Dissolve lime gelatin and salt in the 1 cup hot water in a medium-size bowl; stir in vinegar. Chill about 20 minutes, or until gelatin is as thick as unbeaten egg white.

5 Make fancy topping this way: Set a 6-cup tube mold in a larger bowl or pan partly filled with ice and water to speed setting. Pour ½ cup chicken-broth mixture from Step 2 into mold; chill 5 minutes, or until sticky-soft. Stand halved cucumber slices, rind side down, in gelatin to form a pattern; carefully spoon 1 cup of remaining chicken-broth mixture over. Chill until sticky-firm. Press saved 12 shrimps into gelatin around edge of mold; pour in remaining ½ cup chicken-broth mixture. Chill until sticky-firm.

6 Finish cucumber layer: Blend sour cream and mayonnaise or salad dressing into thickened lime gelatin from Step 4; fold in chopped cucumber. Spoon over shrimp layer in mold. Remove mold from ice and water. Chill at least 3 hours, or until firm. (Overnight is even better.)

7 Just before serving, run a sharp-tip, thin-blade knife around top of mold, then dip mold *very quickly* in and out of a pan of hot water. Invert onto serving plate; carefully lift off mold. Garnish with TOMATO TOPPERS. Serve with marinated shrimps in a separate bowl.

Note: This recipe can be doubled perfectly to make 12 party servings. Make it in a 12-cup mold.

TOMATO TOPPERS—Remove stems from firm cherry tomatoes, allowing one for each serving. Using a sharp-tip, thin-blade knife, score blossom ends halfway down tomato, just through skin, making 5 or 6 cuts; place in a small bowl. Pour boiling water over; let stand 1 minute, then drain. Carefully peel back skin to make petals; top each tomato with a ripe-olive dot. Place on a wooden pick, then stick pick into a lemon wedge.

●

Jellied Chicken Loaf
A perfect keeper, and wonderfully cool eating on a blistery-hot day.
Makes 6 servings

1 broiler-fryer (about 2½ pounds)
  Few celery leaves
1 small onion, sliced
2 teaspoons salt
1 teaspoon ground ginger
8 peppercorns
2 cups water (for chicken)
1 envelope unflavored gelatin
¼ cup cold water (for gelatin)
¼ cup mayonnaise or salad dressing
2 teaspoons soy sauce
½ cup finely diced celery
2 tablespoons finely chopped walnuts

1 Place chicken, celery leaves, onion, salt, ginger, peppercorns, and the 2 cups water in a large saucepan; cover. Heat to boiling, then simmer 1 hour, or until chicken is tender.

2 Remove from broth; cool while fixing gelatin mixture. Strain broth into a 2-cup measure; add water, if needed, to make 2 cups; return to same saucepan.

3 Soften gelatin in the ¼ cup cold water in a 1-cup measure; stir into broth. Heat, stirring constantly, just until gelatin dissolves; stir in mayonnaise or salad dressing and soy sauce.

4 Pour into a 6-cup bowl or mold; chill until as thick as unbeaten egg white.

5 While gelatin mixture chills, remove chicken from bones; chop meat very fine. (There should be about 2¼ cups.) Stir into chilled gelatin mixture with celery and walnuts. Chill several hours, or until firm.

6 Just before serving, run a sharp-tip, thin-blade knife around top of bowl or mold, then dip bowl *very quickly* in and out of a pan of hot water. Invert onto serving plate; carefully lift off bowl. Garnish with crisp lettuce and sliced tomatoes, and serve with crusty French bread or toasted hard rolls.

Molded Corned-Beef Ring
Three favorites—corned beef, cabbage, and potatoes—go fancy in this summery salad.
Makes 6 servings

Corned-Beef Layer
2 envelopes unflavored gelatin
2 tablespoons sugar
3 cups water
2 beef-bouillon cubes
½ cup cider vinegar
1 can (12 ounces) corned beef
  OR: 2 cups diced cooked corned beef
2 cups chopped celery
¼ cup chopped green pepper
1 tablespoon prepared horseradish

Potato-Salad Layer

4 cups diced, peeled, cooked potatoes
2 cups finely shredded cabbage
1 small onion, chopped (¼ cup)
¼ cup chopped parsley
½ cup mayonnaise or salad dressing
½ cup dairy sour cream
1 teaspoon prepared mustard
1 teaspoon salt

1 Make corned-beef layer: Combine gelatin and sugar in a medium-size saucepan; stir in 1 cup of the water and bouillon cubes. Heat, stirring constantly, until gelatin and bouillon cubes dissolve. Remove from heat; stir in remaining 2 cups water and vinegar to mix well.

2 Measure ¾ cup into a small bowl; let stand at room temperature for Step 4. Pour remaining gelatin mixture into a large bowl; chill 30 minutes, or until as thick as unbeaten egg white.

3 Mash canned corned beef lightly with a fork, then stir into thickened gelatin with celery, green pepper, and horseradish. Spoon into a 10-cup ring mold; chill just until sticky-firm.

4 While corned-beef layer chills, make potato-salad layer: Combine potatoes, cabbage, onion, and parsley in a large bowl. Blend mayonnaise or salad dressing, sour cream, mustard, and salt into the ¾ cup gelatin from Step 2; fold into potato mixture.

5 Spoon over sticky-firm corned-beef layer in mold; chill at least 4 hours, or until firm.

6 Just before serving, run a sharp-tip, thin-blade knife around top of mold, then dip mold *very quickly* in and out of a pan of hot water. Invert onto serving plate; carefully lift off mold. Garnish plate with salad greens and serve with additional mayonnaise or salad dressing, if you wish.

Salmon Supper Mold

Freshly cooked salmon steak is the star of this fluffy main-dish salad.
Makes 6 servings

1 fresh or frozen salmon steak (about ¾ pound)
4 peppercorns
1 teaspoon salt
1 slice of lemon
1 slice of onion
Handful of celery leaves
Water
1 envelope unflavored gelatin
1 envelope instant vegetable broth
1½ cups water
1 teaspoon grated onion
1 teaspoon lemon juice
⅛ teaspoon pepper

OR: Few drops liquid red pepper seasoning
½ cup mayonnaise or salad dressing
1 cup chopped celery

1 Simmer salmon steak with peppercorns, ½ teaspoon salt, lemon and onion slices, and celery leaves in just enough water to cover in a medium-size frying pan, 15 minutes, or until salmon flakes easily with a fork.

2 Lift out carefully with a slotted spatula; drain on paper toweling until cool enough to handle, then remove skin and bones. Flake salmon; place in a small bowl. (There should be about 1½ cups.) Set aside for Step 4.

3 Soften gelatin with vegetable broth in 1 cup of the water in a medium-size saucepan; heat, stirring constantly, just until gelatin dissolves. Stir in remaining ½ cup water, onion, lemon juice, remaining ½ teaspoon salt, pepper or red pepper seasoning. Chill 30 to 40 minutes, or until as thick as unbeaten egg white.

4 Stir in mayonnaise or salad dressing; fold in salmon and celery. Spoon into a 4-cup mold; chill several hours, or until firm.

5 Just before serving, run a sharp-tip, thin-blade knife around top of mold, then dip mold *very quickly* in and out of a pan of hot water. Invert onto serving plate; carefully lift off mold. Serve with lemon wedges to squeeze over, or with your favorite bottled tartare sauce, if you wish.

Redcap Veal Mousse

Tomato-aspic layer atop creamy-light veal salad makes this most inviting main dish.
Makes 6 to 8 servings

Tomato-Aspic Layer

1 envelope unflavored gelatin
1 cup water
1 can (8 ounces) tomato sauce
1 teaspoon lemon juice

Veal Layer

1 envelope unflavored gelatin
1 cup water
1 can (10½ ounces) condensed cream of celery soup
¼ cup mayonnaise or salad dressing
2 cups chopped cooked veal
¼ cup chopped toasted almonds (from a 5-ounce can)
1 tablespoon chopped parsley
1 teaspoon chopped chives

635

1 Make tomato-aspic layer: Soften gelatin in water in a small saucepan; heat, stirring constantly, just until gelatin dissolves; remove from heat.

2 Blend in tomato sauce and lemon juice; pour into an 8-cup mold; chill just until sticky-firm.

3 While tomato-aspic layer chills, make veal layer: Soften gelatin in water in a medium-size saucepan; heat, stirring constantly, just until gelatin dissolves. Stir in soup until mixture is smooth; remove from heat.

4 Blend in mayonnaise or salad dressing, then stir in veal, almonds, parsley , and chives. Chill until as thick as unbeaten egg white.

5 Spoon over tomato-aspic layer in mold; chill several hours, or until firm.

6 Just before serving, run a sharp-tip, thin-blade knife around top of mold, then dip mold *very quickly* in and out of a pan of hot water. Invert onto serving plate; carefully lift off mold. Garnish with lemon wedges, and serve with additional mayonnaise or salad dressing, if you wish.

BEAT THE HEAT WITH— FROSTY LIGHT DESSERTS

Party Almond Cheese Mold
This rich-rich dessert from the Old World is traditionally pyramid shape. We used a plastic flowerpot for our mold.
Makes 12 to 16 servings

2 packages (8 ounces each) cream cheese
½ cup (1 stick) butter or margarine
1 cup 10X (confectioners' powdered) sugar
1 egg
1 teaspoon vanilla
½ cup finely chopped toasted slivered almonds (from a 5-ounce can)
¼ cup finely chopped citron

1 Put cream cheese and butter or margarine in a medium-size bowl; set aside to soften while preparing mold.

2 Wash and dry a plastic flowerpot about 5 inches in diameter, or a 1-pound coffee can with holes punched in the bottom. (Holes are necessary so cheese mixture can drain as it chills.) Cut a piece of double-thick cheesecloth large

enough to line mold and hang over edge; wring out in cold water; line mold. Set aside for Step 4.

3 Beat 10X sugar into cream cheese and butter until fluffy; beat in egg and vanilla; fold in almonds and citron.

4 Spoon into prepared mold, smoothing top to make even. (Mixture may not fill flowerpot.) Cover tightly with wax paper or transparent wrap; place on a plate to catch liquid that seeps out. Chill overnight.

5 To serve, remove paper. Cover mold with a serving plate; turn upside down; lift off mold. Carefully peel off cheesecloth.

6 Cut into thin wedges, for it's very rich. Serve with fresh berries (raspberries, strawberries, blackberries, blueberries), sliced fresh peaches or pineapple, or stewed fresh plums.

636

A cooling quintet: Party Almond Cheese-Mold, Lime Angel Pouf Pie, Lemon Ruffle, Candy-Stick Meltaway and Watermelon Jewel with melon-ball kebabs.

Lime Angel Pouf Pie

Big dollops of cream billow high atop the fluffiest tangiest chiffon filling.

Bake at 425° for 15 minutes. Makes one 9-inch pie

1 package piecrust mix
1 cup sugar
1 envelope unflavored gelatin
¼ teaspoon salt
½ teaspoon vanilla
4 eggs, separated
½ cup water
¼ cup lime juice
2 teaspoons grated lime rind
1 cup cream for whipping
2 tablespoons 10X (confectioners' powdered) sugar

1 Prepare piecrust mix, following label directions, or make pastry from your own favorite one-crust recipe. Roll out to a 12-inch round on lightly floured pastry cloth or board; fit into a 9-inch pie plate. Trim overhang to ½ inch; turn under flush with rim; flute to make a stand-up edge. Prick shell well all over with a fork.

2 Bake in hot oven (425°) 15 minutes, or until golden; cool completely on wire rack before filling.

3 Combine ½ cup sugar, gelatin, salt, and vanilla in top of a double boiler. (Save remaining ½ cup sugar for Step 6.)

4 Beat egg yolks slightly in a small bowl; stir in water and lime juice; stir into gelatin mixture.

5 Cook, stirring constantly, over simmering water, 10 minutes, or until gelatin dissolves and

mixture coats a metal spoon. Strain into a small bowl; stir in lime rind. Chill, stirring several times, until mixture is as thick as unbeaten egg white.

6 Beat egg whites until foamy-white and double in volume in a large bowl; sprinkle in saved ½ cup sugar, 1 tablespoon at a time, beating all the time until sugar completely dissolves and meringue stands in firm peaks.

7 Place bowl of meringue in a larger bowl or pan partly filled with ice and water. Spoon thickened gelatin mixture on top; carefully fold in, keeping bowl over ice, until no streaks of white remain and mixture mounds on a spoon.

8 Spoon into cooled pastry shell; chill 3 to 4 hours, or until firm.

9 Just before serving, beat cream and 10X sugar until stiff in a medium-size bowl; drop by teaspoonfuls onto filling to form a crown. Sprinkle with additional grated lime rind, if you wish.

Watermelon Jewel
It's a glittering, pretty-to-look-at dessert with a most refreshing flavor.
Makes 4 servings

 1 *package (3 ounces) raspberry-flavor gelatin*
  Water
 1 *tablespoon lime juice*
 ⅔ *cup small watermelon balls*

1 Prepare gelatin with water in a small bowl, following label directions; stir in lime juice. Pour into 4 parfait glasses.

2 Thread 7 or 8 watermelon balls on each of 4 long wooden picks; place a pick in each glass. Chill several hours, or until firm. Serve plain, or with a spoonful of dairy sour cream, if you wish.

638

Candy-Stick Meltaway
Spoon into this shimmery dessert, and you'll find a surprise minty-sweet syrup.
Makes 4 servings

 1 *package (3 ounces) lime-flavor gelatin*
  Water
 4 *green peppermint sticks, each about 3 inches long*

1 Prepare gelatin with water in a small bowl, following label directions. Chill until as thick as unbeaten egg white.

2 Spoon into 4 six-ounce parfait glasses or custard cups, dividing evenly.

3 Carefully push a peppermint stick deep into gelatin in each glass. (If using custard cups, break peppermint sticks in half.)

4 Chill several hours, or until gelatin is firm. (Peppermint sticks dissolve to form a sweet syrup in the center of each dessert.)

5 Serve plain or with a dollop of whipped cream, if you wish.

Lemon Ruffle
Each serving has its sauce—a tiny cone of lemony cream cheese—molded in the center.
Makes 4 servings

 1 *package (3 ounces) lemon-flavor gelatin*
  Water
 1 *package (3 or 4 ounces) cream cheese*
 2 *tablespoons 10X (confectioners' powdered) sugar*
 1 *teaspoon grated lemon rind*

1 Prepare gelatin with water in a small bowl, following label directions. Chill until as thick as unbeaten egg white.

2 While gelatin chills, blend cream cheese, 10X sugar, and lemon rind in a small bowl; spoon into a pastry bag; attach plain tip.

3 Spoon 2 tablespoons chilled gelatin into each of 4 six-ounce stemmed glasses or custard cups. Chill 5 minutes, or until softly set. Keep remaining gelatin at room temperature while making cheese cones.

4 Press cream-cheese mixture, using a circular motion, through pastry bag on top of gelatin layer in each glass to form a cone. (Or you can simply spoon about a tablespoonful of cream-cheese mixture in a mound on top of layer.)

5 Spoon remaining gelatin carefully, dividing evenly, around cheese cone. Chill several hours, or until firm.

LIST OF RECIPES IN VOLUME V